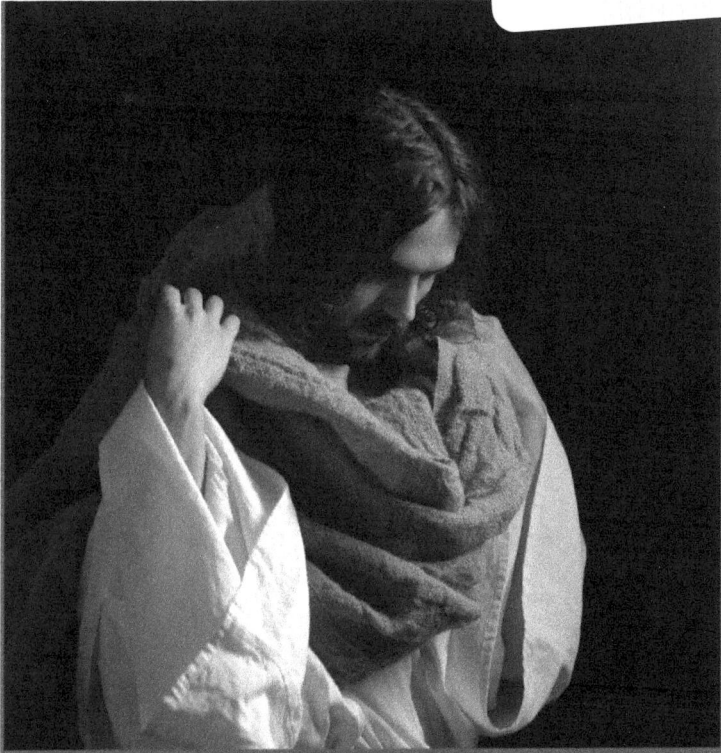

The Jeremiah Generation

God's Response to Injustice

Jeanne Metcalf

1st Publication 2021
2nd Publication 2022

Cëgullah Publishing & Apologetic Academy (CP & AA)
3rd Publication International Copyright © 2025
www.cegullahpublishing.ca

ISBN # Textbook: 978-1-926489-36-0

ISBN # Workbook: 978-1-926489-39-1

Cover photo © iStock # 1158248984 (2021)
Cover design by Jeanne Metcalf.

SCRIPTURE MATTERS

Many scholars challenge newer versions of scripture for their accuracy. Therefore, in the interests of being accurate, we chose to use the oldest version of scripture, the KJV. While there are many accuracy challenges within this version too, we find it much easier to validate original language words and thus authenticate accuracy. We have also noted that once a person becomes familiar with the KJV it becomes a little easier to understand. Therefore, all quotes in this book originate from the KJV, *except the name of God appears as YHVH (yod, heh, vav, heh) or YeHoVaH.* See Appendix for more information about the reason for this change.

---

[1] See Contact Page in Appendix.

DEDICATION

To all prophetic voices called to speak the oracles of Almighty God to their generation, especially those called within the Jeremiah Generation, **I dedicate this book.**

It is my prayer, for each one who speaks boldly for God, that the powerful and burning fire of the Almighty's presence possesses your reigns.

May every prophet stand tall in their generation, especially, those called to stand in the Jeremiah Generation!

COURSE 705

THE JEREMIAH GENERATION

SECTION 1: INJUSTICE – ROOTED

- *People & Promiscuous Times*

Matters of:

COURSE 801

THE JEREMIAH GENERATION

SECTION 2: INJUSTICE - REFUTED

- *Prophet & Powerful Message*

Matters of:

SECTION 3: INJUSTICE - REMOVED

- *Punishment & Promised Restoration*

Matters of:

APPENDIX

COURSE 705

The Jeremiah Generation

INTRODUCTION

INTRODUCTION

"To everything there is a season, and a time to every purpose under the heaven: "

Ecclesiastes 3:1

YeHoVaH,[2] is Eternal. He lives forever. Human beings, however, do not. We live for a season, a certain segment of time, and then, we pass away from this world. Our time on this earth, however long or short, whenever categorized collectively with other people alive at the same time, we call a generation.

Generations since the early 1900's received certain names. For example, the Silent Generation consists of those in the mid 1920's to the end of World War II, about a 20-year time span. As that generation bore children, their offspring became known as the Baby Boomers. The children of the Baby Boomers we call Generation X, the children of Generation X we call Xennials. Coming to the current timeframe, we classify the generation born anywhere from 2013 to 2025 as Gen-Alpha, or Generation Alpha[3].

---

[2] See Appendix for the understanding of this Name and its use.
[3] Dates are approximate. For a more accurate description regarding timelines, try investigating the web.

Naming generations, while not a new thing, categorizes or measures a certain culture, helping to define responses of behaviour within their cultural setting. From an analysis, we therefore walk away with ideas of how they reacted in one generation compared to another. For example, by looking at the Silent Generation as they came through the Second World War, we see how their daily lives changed as they walked through their experiences from before the war to after. By examining the long and short-term changes in their culture, hopefully we learn from their experiences, especially their pitfalls.

Looking at generations to analyze their spiritual values helps us to determine their spiritual temperature to the Creator. Looking at the Silent Generation during the Second World War period, we easily identify their confrontation with their own mortality. With some, their affection and trust in God increased, while others abandoned any idea of God's existence. Many of such persuasion blamed God for the disasters they experienced. Indeed, looking at various responses of individuals, both male and female, on and off the front lines, we recognize either the development of a deeper, stronger faith in God by some individuals, as

---

Careerplanner.com, at last investigation, had an excellent recap of the generations since the 1890's.

compared to others who deny, abandon, or defame any form of a belief system.[4]

That Silent Generation, as well as others who faced death, either by war, disease, or plague in other generations, bring out a variety of responses, especially when confronted with their own mortality or that of their loved ones. Many seniors of that generation, as well as others from more recent generations, who have a lifetime of living under their belt, find themselves nodding in agreement with the wisdom of the one who authored this beautiful summary of life:

Ecclesiastes 3:1-8

> *"1 ¶ To every thing there is a season, and a time to every purpose under the heaven: 2 A time to be born, and a time to die; a time to plant, and a time to pluck up that which is planted; 3 A time to kill, and a time to heal; a time to break down, and a time to build up; 4 A time to weep, and a time to laugh; a time to mourn, and a time to dance; 5 A time to cast away stones, and a time to gather*

---

[4] Here, you will not find quotes from the Silent Generation, however, as a Baby Boomer many stories of the 2nd World War, from relatives of the Silent Generation, dotted my youth. Stories of soldiers who drew close to God and experienced miracles came into my listening ears, as well as stories of their friends or companions who ran from God. I heard stories of those who faced death, and either died in great fear or barely escaped the jaws of death. There were tales related of last-minute choices about God on the battle front. These permanently altered their concept of God; some for good and some for bad. This gave me much information on their perception of their generation, and how many of them responded to God in it!

stones together; a time to embrace, and a time to refrain from embracing; 6 A time to get, and a time to lose; a time to keep, and a time to cast away; 7 A time to rend, and a time to sew; a time to keep silence, and a time to speak; 8 A time to love, and a time to hate; a time of war, and a time of peace."

Indeed, to every generation there is a set time under heaven for them. Within the timeframe of their generational setting, they chart a course and set sail upon it! Often, one generation will learn from another, especially, as they examine the mistakes of a previous generation, and desperately wish to avoid them.

Examining the Silent Generation and their children, the Baby Boomers, we recognize a determination arose within them to do all in their power to avert another World War. Peace became paramount. Their firsthand experience cautioned them to focus away from pathways leading to more horrors of war! Thus, in speaking to their children and grandchildren, they kept fresh in their mind that the 2nd World War killed more than 35 million[5] and disabled more than 20 million people.[6] That aspect of history, in their minds, best not repeat itself.

---

[5] This figure includes those who died after the war from things that took place during the war.

[6] "howmanyarethere.net".

Truly, if we take time to look and see, we might glean much from former generations. If we become ardent students of that generation, indeed, we will discover mindsets which we desire to follow, or to avoid in our own generation. Taking the time to look back may furnish us with lessons to change our future for the better. Past generation reflection highlights decisions our ancestors made, and the calamities or escapes that touched their lives.

Seeing the errors in the former generations, and understanding the platform that led to the failures, opened a door, which brought forth insights to avoid repeating history. Those detrimental past events, when thoroughly understood, became markers or buoys to point out dangerous waters to the people of future generations.

In short, when humankind takes the time to look at previous generations and study their behaviour, gaining wisdom from the mistakes made in earlier generations, great possibilities arise for avoiding the same devastating experiences. This is one fantastic reason to study history!

Moving past secular history, now, to biblical history, we have even more empowering lessons. To study Biblical history with their generations, pointers highlight the spiritual errors of former generations, such as those who received God's judgments for their ungodly ways.

In Psalm 78:1-8 we hear the Psalmist's wisdom relate to both current and future generations admonishing them. He is especially mindful of understanding what keeps them in their days of prosperity. He advises them to carefully watch their days as they live them within the covenant setting YeHoVaH, the God of Israel, gave to His People:

Psalm 78:1-3
"1 Give ear, O my people, [to] my law: incline your ears to the words of my mouth. 2 I will open my mouth in a parable: I will utter dark sayings of old: 3 Which we have heard and known, and our fathers have told us. "

Here begins the wisdom of the former generation related, beginning with these words *"what the fathers have told us"*:

Psalm 78:4-5
"4 We will not hide [them] from their children, shewing to the generation to come the praises of YeHoVaH, and his strength, and his wonderful works that he hath done. 5 For he established a testimony in Jacob, and appointed a law[7] in Israel, which he

---

[7] Word here is Torah, meaning instructions.

commanded our fathers, that they should make them known to their children: "

Here we see that YeHoVaH commanded them to make known His Instructions. In the following verses we hear clear evidence as to why:

Psalm 78:6-8

*"6 That the generation **to come**[8] might know [them, even] the children [which] should be born; [who] should arise and declare [them] to their children: 7 **That they might set their hope in God, and not forget the works of God, but keep his commandments:** 8 And might not be as their fathers, a stubborn and rebellious generation; a generation [that] set not their heart aright, and whose spirit was not stedfast with God."*

Truly, the truth of this scripture rings home as genuine, God-based wisdom. If Israel is to survive, then the generation to come must set their hope in YeHoVaH. They must not forget His works, and they must keep His commandments.

If the future generations followed this advice, they would __not__ become a generation of stubborn and rebellious people, who never set the course of their heart true north to follow YeHoVaH. Their spirit within them, to find hope and a future in God, must

---

[8] Author bolded and italicized the text.

adhere and be faithful to YeHoVaH. Thus, the next generation would follow behaviours of which YeHoVaH approved and consequently, avoid the horrible consequences of earlier generations, who walked in profound disobedience and rebellion. This is the best result of reviewing history and from it, relaying realities to another generation! If they embrace the wisdom, their lives will see the realization of greater blessing!

Such is the desired end of those who wish to glean powerful lessons from the historical account of Israel, found within the pages of the book of Jeremiah[9]. These inhabitants of the land during that time, we might classify as the "Jeremiah Generation". That generation in Israel's history experienced the harsh hand of God's Judgment for their negligence and blatant sin against God, as they disregarded His Commandments and Precepts.

These offences began generations earlier; however, some repentance did occur, which delayed the hand of God's Judgment. Once we arrive at Jeremiah's lifetime, however, we discover a generation lost in

---

[9] To study the entire book of Jeremiah would take a long time. While in this course you are invited to read the entire book of Jeremiah, the course covers only highlights of that book, focusing on the people of that generation.

aimless, senseless, even forbidden religious activities, traditions, and cultural activities, which deeply offended YeHoVaH.

To study their behaviour and response to God's prophet, Jeremiah, we find vivid glimpses of how YeHoVaH handled that generation, including the remarkable prophetic voice, Jeremiah, He sent to call that generation to return to Him. Jeremiah, God's merciful emissary, this powerful gift from God, experienced mistreatment and abuse at their hands. Nevertheless, Jeremiah remained steadfast in God's love and continued to declare God's Word. With God's help, he confronted that generation, pointing out the many injustices they committed, proclaiming God's viewpoint. He warned them that, without repentance, they could not escape or avoid the day of accountability.

In this study, The Jeremiah Generation, we'll expose the roots of injustice operative in the land of Israel at that time. As we do, watch for the shift of authority from the Word of God to the word of man. Then, look to see how things quickly degraded, even though God, constantly, called them to return to Him.

In examining Jeremiah's life, looking at the prophet's credentials, the problems he faced, and the many obstacles requiring an overcoming faith in God, we will learn what it takes to stand in such a time as that of Jeremiah's generation. In addition, we will see God's drastic measures necessary to implement in order to remove the injustice, so operative in the Jeremiah Generation. In the final moments of this study, we will highlight the necessary conclusions to bring this information past Jeremiah's day into ours, making this message relevant to our times.

Hopefully, with an analysis of our own generation in front of us, we will recognize the proximity of our generation to that of the Jeremiah Generation: *the one of God's judgment.* Are we *nearing that generation or are we living in it?*

Precious reader let us join our hearts together, and pray for students and teacher, alike, to receive ears to hear, eyes to see and a heart to perceive the generation in which we live. *May each of us recognize God's call to stand for righteousness and truth within our generation, willing to pay the cost to present God's Word, whether our generation exists before, after or within that generation of God's judgment, namely, that of:*

The Jeremiah Generation.

The Jeremiah Generation

SECTION 1:

INJUSTICE ROOTED

(People & Promiscuous Times)

MATTERS OF
MATERIALISTIC MINDSETS

1

"Have not I commanded thee? Be strong and of a good courage; be not afraid, neither be thou dismayed: for YeHoVaH thy God [is] with thee whithersoever thou goest."

Joshua 1:9

In every walk of life, mindsets make a difference. An engineer with a creative nature may excel in architectural building designs, however, unless he or she sticks to basic structural rules, that finished masterpiece might not stand the test of weather or time. The creative mindset must align with architectural realities.

Likewise, the scientist, experimenting with the elements of this earth, may explore creative ideas to present mankind with a never-before seen invention, however, they too must keep their process of experimentation within certain parameters of earth's realities. For example, the atom bomb in its early developmental stage promised to end a world war, however, its use caused great devastation. Without restricted mindsets aligning its continued use within the parameters of humane management, this scientific invention holds enough power to destroy the earth and all living in it. Humane mindsets, here, matter greatly!

Looking at mindsets, worldwide, we know that individuals living within any given country do not all hold the same mindsets. Certainly, people, regardless of their upbringing, society, and its moral values, or other influential forces upon their life, think contrary to one another. For instance, a person raised in Communist China, who aligns with that regime's policies allowing that regime to form their mindsets, reacts totally different to a similar person living in Communist China, who does not agree with that regime's guidelines. Individual mindsets matter, especially when two people wish to walk together as friends. Opposite mindsets interfere with unity.

SPIRITUALLY SPEAKING:

Let us move this scenario now to the arena of spirituality. Think about the children of Israel exiting from centuries of slavery in Egypt. What mindsets did they possess? What mindsets challenged them as they walked away from all they knew in Egypt as they headed towards the Promised Land? Once in the Promised Land, mindsets, again, needed to change for them to grasp the concept of taking and holding that land for themselves. Our opening scripture gives us an example of a mindset Joshua must embrace:

Joshua 1:9

"9 Have not I commanded thee? Be strong and of a good courage; be not afraid, neither be thou dismayed: for YeHoVaH thy God [is] with thee whithersoever thou goest. "

In looking at surrounding scripture, we find a description of their present reality, the challenge ahead, as well as YeHoVaH's instructions to Joshua:

Joshua 1:1-8

"1 Now after the death of Moses the servant of YeHoVaH it came to pass, that YeHoVaH spake unto Joshua the son of Nun, Moses' minister, saying, 2 Moses my servant is dead; now therefore arise, go over this Jordan, thou, and all this people, unto the land which I do give to them, [even] to the children of Israel.

3 Every place that the sole of your foot shall tread upon, that have I given unto you, as I said unto Moses. 4 From the wilderness and this Lebanon even unto the great river, the river Euphrates, all the land of the Hittites, and unto the great sea toward the going down of the sun, shall be your coast.

5 There shall not any man be able to stand before thee all the days of thy life: as I was with Moses, [so] I will be with thee: I will not fail thee, nor forsake thee. 6 Be strong and of a good courage: for unto this people shalt

*thou divide for an inheritance the land, which I sware
unto their fathers to give them.*

*7 Only be thou strong and very courageous, that thou
mayest observe to do according to all the law, which
Moses my servant commanded thee: turn not from it
[to] the right hand or [to] the left, that thou mayest
prosper whithersoever thou goest. 8 This book of the
law shall not depart out of thy mouth; but thou shalt
meditate therein day and night, that thou mayest
observe to do according to all that is written therein:
for then thou shalt make thy way prosperous, and then
thou shalt have good success. "*

Moses, the great leader of the Israelites, died. Joshua,
his successor, must lead the children of Israel forward
into the Promised Land. Yet, this was not a simple
task. *It meant war!*

Were the Israelites raised for confrontation in their
environment? Were they trained to move directly
forward, head on into conflicts with the Egyptians to
remove them if they impeded their goals? Hardly! The
Israelites, including Joshua, lived as slaves within the
Egyptian Empire.

As an enslaved people they had a subjugated mindset.
Egypt oppressed, demeaned, and forced them to do
the will of Pharaoh. That subjugated mindset must

change if they are to enter the Promised Land and live as conquerors!

A mindset change must, indeed, take place! They must rise above the thinking of their earlier situation in Egypt. To embrace the freedom they desired, they must learn to live free, including to embrace the mindsets that overcome the slave mentality.

After the death of Moses, YeHoVaH chose a new leader amongst them, one who, under Moses, made the transition from forced slavery to true liberty, willingly serving the Most High God in holiness. After the death of Moses, God calls Joshua to arise and come to the front. He must become like a polished shaft in the hand of the living God and fearlessly lead the people of Israel into the Promised Land.

FIRST ASSIGNMENT: CROSS A RIVER!

After living 40 years in the wilderness, Joshua stood ready to enter the Promise Land with an entirely new generation of people at the forefront with him. His first assignment: cross a river. No boats, no rafts, no easy way of crossing lay in front of them! Joshua had only the command of YeHoVaH, but it was enough:

Joshua 1:2
> *"2 Moses my servant is dead; now therefore arise, go over this Jordan, thou, and all this people, unto the land which I do give to them, [even] to the children of Israel."*

God's word was enough! Joshua obeyed:

Joshua 1:3
> *"3 Every place that the sole of your foot shall tread upon, that have I given unto you, as I said unto Moses. "*

Thus, Joshua moved forward, the soles of his feet touching what was in front of him. The waters parted as he implemented the plans of YeHoVaH!

As Joshua lived out his life, we see he never forgot God's declarations or commands:

- No man will be able to stand before you all the days of your life: as I was with Moses, [so] I will be with you: I will not fail you, nor forsake you. (vs 5)
- Be strong and of a good courage: for unto this people shalt thou divide for an inheritance the land, which I swore unto their fathers to give them. (vs 6)
- Only be strong and very courageous, that you may observe to do according to all the law, which Moses my servant commanded you: turn

not from it [to] the right hand or [to] the left, that you may prosper wherever you go. (vs7)

- This book of the law shall not depart out of your mouth; but you shall meditate therein day and night, that you may observe to do according to all that is written therein: for then you shall make your way prosperous, and then you shall have good success. (vs 8)

Joshua lived by these instructions, as did some of the great heroes of the faith. However, far too many of God's people ignored them and did their own thing. Many embraced mindsets of their own culture and day in which they lived. Such was the way of the Jeremiah Generation.

JEREMIAH'S GENERATION:

Those in the time of Jeremiah, including kings, nobles, rich merchants and so many others refused to see things God's way. Rather, they clung to the mindsets of former idolatrous and rebellious generations, continuing to embrace what they learned from their parents and grandparents. Their developed mindsets were like brick walls which Jeremiah confronted, continually. In fact, in Jeremiah's lengthy forty-year ministry as he challenged government and people to forsake their ways and embrace God's, he saw little to no fruit[10]. His passionately prophesied prophetic words fell on deaf ears.

As we walk, together, through this study, the various mindsets embraced by the children of Judah as they lived in the days prior to the Babylonian captivity will arise. When they do, we will see how they clung to mindsets taught to them by multiple, former generations. Also, we will see how they fully accepted the false prophets who encouraged the keeping of those mindsets of their forefathers. We will see how Jeremiah challenged those mindsets and the people's response to his confrontations.

You might wish to brace yourself, too, as you study the Jeremiah generation. In that society, at that timeframe, the people, affected by their very prosperous living, grew cold to the needs of the poor around them. So hardened by their sin, they stayed within their forged mindsets, refusing to change. Both government and people, approved of the sacrifice of infant children offered to Molech, thus spilling the blood of those innocent babes throughout God's land, even in Jerusalem!

---

[10] Some Jewish sources say Jeremiah prophesied for 40 years, while other sources accredit him with more years and some less. For the sake of this book, we will consider it 40 years.

Jeremiah, sent by YeHoVaH, deadlocked against their thinking, confronted them, and suffered as they rejected his call and his word, as they beat him, imprisoned him, and at one point, left him to die in a muddy, old cistern. While YeHoVaH's hand rescued Jeremiah occasion after occasion, Jeremiah's message continued to fall on deaf ears. That Jeremiah generation refused to heed the call of God! They forsook God's timeless principles for doing things God's way. Rather, they exchanged those holy concepts of God for doing things their way, often reasoning away the Words of YeHoVaH!

MINDSETS CHALLENGED BY GOD:

This people of the Jeremiah generation, called of God to be like Him, were anything but! Therefore, Jeremiah, under God's direction, challenged them to return to God, to function as He destined them to function. God called them out for Himself as a people to represent Him on the earth and through Jeremiah challenged them to forsake their godless mindsets and align with the One Who gave them life.

As you read Jeremiah, you will see that God promised His Presence to accompany him. In many ways, His promise to Jeremiah looked a lot like the one given to Moses!

Jeremiah 1:17-19

"17 Thou therefore gird up thy loins, and arise, and speak unto them all that I command thee: be not dismayed at their faces, lest I confound thee before them. 18 For, behold, I have made thee this day a defenced city, and an iron pillar, and brasen walls against the whole land, against the kings of Judah, against the princes thereof, against the priests thereof, and against the people of the land. 19 And they shall fight against thee; but they shall not prevail against thee; for I [am] with thee, saith YeHoVaH, to deliver thee. "

In short, remembering to obey God's Word and face every situation with His Presence with us, ensures our success in God's eyes. It is not likely you will find these principles quoted in a journal on how to succeed, today. Nevertheless, even in our time, the timeless message still calls from the pages of scripture.[11] God saw to their placement for the admonition and learning of those who wish to follow the ways of the Almighty One of Israel. To do that, mindset adjustments may be necessary, repeatedly, until we grasp the deeper meaning of God's blueprint for success.

---

[11] *2 Timothy 3:16-17 "All scripture [is] given by inspiration of God, and [is] profitable for doctrine, for reproof, for correction, for instruction in righteousness: 17 That the man of God may be perfect, thoroughly furnished unto all good works. "*

In doing so, we slowly come out of agreement with those former mindsets, which spoke contrary ideas to those of the Word of God. However, if Moses, Joshua, and others forsook the godless ideas of their world in which they were raised, and learned to walk in a godly, empowering mindset, so can we!

MATTERS OF
RULING ROYALS

2

"1 The words of Jeremiah the son of Hilkiah, of the priests that were in Anathoth in the land of Benjamin: 2 To whom the word of YeHoVaH came in the days of Josiah the son of Amon king of Judah, in the thirteenth year of his reign. 3 It came also in the days of Jehoiakim the son of Josiah king of Judah, unto the end of the eleventh year of Zedekiah the son of Josiah king of Judah, unto the carrying away of Jerusalem captive in the fifth month. "

Jeremiah 1:1-3

Jeremiah begins his discourse with clear reference to the times in which he prophesied, thus outlining the times of his ministry. It began in the 13th year of King Josiah and continued until Babylon broke down the walls of Jerusalem, destroyed the Temple and took many captives to Babylon. Later Jeremiah, taken forcibly by the people to Egypt, continued to prophecy until the people stoned him to death in about 570 BCE[12].

---

[12] That date, BCE (Before Common Era), comes from secular scholars. Jewish scholars have very different dates!

In reviewing Jeremiah's prophecies, which he uttered for a little over 40 years, we discover that he began to speak as religious reforms sprang up in Judah. These reforms arose by order of Josiah, the King of Judah. Josiah began to reign at the age of 8 and reigned for 31 years, dying in a battle against the King of Egypt.

During Josiah's reign, Hilkiah the high priest, under orders to restore the temple, discovered a scroll containing the book of Deuteronomy. This book helped Judah to see her backslidden state and set the king on a course to realign Judah with God's plans for the nation. Josiah, in his reign, brought back the practice of Passover, and aimed a strong hand to remove the worship of the Baals[13] from the land of Judah, for many of the people held to such idolatrous beliefs.

Jeremiah began prophesying in Josiah's reign, approximately, 18 years before Josiah died. Thus, the mood of the king and kingdom, when Jeremiah began his ministry, pointed towards a call to reform and repentance. Even so amidst the call, the scriptures state no positive response to Jeremiah's words, only rejection and retaliation:

---

[13] Baals, worshipped by Israel, Judah and others involved sacrifices to idols, child sacrifice and more.

Jeremiah 1:14-19

> *"14 Then YeHoVaH said unto me, Out of the north an evil shall break forth upon all the inhabitants of the land. 15 For, lo, I will call all the families of the kingdoms of the north, saith YeHoVaH; and they shall come, and they shall set every one his throne at the entering of the gates of Jerusalem, and against all the walls thereof round about, and against all the cities of Judah. 16 And I will utter my judgments against them touching all their wickedness, who have forsaken me, and have burned incense unto other gods, and worshipped the works of their own hands.*
>
> *17 Thou therefore gird up thy loins, and arise, and speak unto them all that I command thee: be not dismayed at their faces, lest I confound thee before them. 18 For, behold, I have made thee this day a defenced city, and an iron pillar, and brasen walls against the whole land, against the kings of Judah, against the princes thereof, against the priests thereof, and against the people of the land. 19 And they shall fight against thee; but they shall not prevail against thee; for I [am] with thee, saith YeHoVaH, to deliver thee. "*

A CALL TO REPENTANCE:

It is obvious from these few scriptures, the people of Judah including the kings, the princes (members of the king's government), the priests (member of the House of God to rule the people) as well as the people, refused the word of YeHoVaH at the mouth of Jeremiah. Jeremiah describes, throughout his prophecies, much detail of YeHoVaH's disappointment and grief with His people.

That stubborn Jeremiah generation refused to allow the convicting power of the Holy Spirit to open their eyes to a relationship with God that greatly fell short of His expectations. They muffled their ears to receive an anointed call to repent and return to God. In short, those of the Jeremiah generation fought against YeHoVaH, His Words and the prophet He sent them to warn of the coming judgment. They chose to keep their sins and iniquities, preferring them over YeHoVaH's call to repentance.

Walking through the book of Jeremiah[14], we hear Jeremiah repeatedly outline and detail great rebellion against God, His statutes, and commandments. In Jeremiah's earlier years of preaching, we hear about King Josiah, who tried to reform Judah, bringing her back to a state of righteousness with YeHoVaH. Before this ground-breaking reformation moved too far along, Josiah, although warned not to engage in a

---

[14] Even though the kings, which are listed within the book of Jeremiah, appear to fall in chronological order some, scholars believe the writings in Jeremiah are not in chronological order.

certain battle, did so. King Josiah died in that battle, one in which Israel had no business to fight.

REFORMATION DIES:

At that point, the reformation and restoration, which King Josiah began in Judah, died along with him. As Jeremiah continued to prophesy, he faced the kings of Judah from Josiah down to the last one, Zedekiah. Constantly, we hear of continued warnings and comments about their rebellion. Eventually, on cue, King Nebuchadnezzar forced his way into the city of Jerusalem, burning the temple. He also foiled King Zedekiah's plan to escape, thus fulfilling the prophecy of Jeremiah to the letter.

King Zedekiah kept his life just as Jeremiah predicted, however, Nebuchadnezzar killed every one of the sons of King Zedekiah, right in front of his very eyes. Then, they blinded Zedekiah to seal forever in his mind the torment of those last moments of his family's life. Zedekiah, again just as Jeremiah prophesied, spent his remaining days in a Babylonian prison. It was there, in Babylon, the last reigning King of Judah died.[15]

---

[15] While the captives, later, returned to Jerusalem, no one sat as King on the throne of David in Jerusalem. While the returning leaders from the tribe of Judah came back, they were subservient rulers to the conquering nation. Today, that throne waits for the true King of Israel to come and sit upon it. The "Tsemach Tsekek"

In summary, Jeremiah prophesied through the reign of:[16]

KING	BEGAN	END[17]	TIME
Josiah	640	609	31 yrs.
Jehoahaz	609	609	3 mos.
Jehoiakim	609	598	11 yrs.
Jehoiachin (Jeconiah)	598	598	3 mos. 10 days
Zedekiah	597	586	11 years

Beginning in the 13th year of Josiah's reign (627 BCE), and prophesying to the end of Zedekiah's reign (586), when Babylon captured Jerusalem, Jeremiah prophesied to Judah for a little over 40 years. During his prophetic ministry, scripture speaks of prophetess Huldah[18], who, according to some sources was a relative of Jeremiah. In addition, Hilkiah the High Priest, some speculate was Jeremiah's father, although some scholars strongly disagree.

(Righteous Branch) Yeshua (Jesus) is the only one worthy to sit upon that throne!

[16] BCE remember you count backwards to year 0!

[17] In accordance with the Gregorian Calendar, found on en.wikipedia.org/wiki/kings of Judah.

[18] 2 Kings 22:14; 2 Chronicles 34:22 speak about Huldah.

A KING AND HIS COURT:

In reading the pages of Jeremiah, it is not hard to notice the challenging confrontations of Jeremiah to the kings, including his court and justice system, along with all aspects of government operating in the nation, secular or religious. Under the government, which the kings set up in Jerusalem and gave nobility a free hand to operate, Jeremiah experienced much abuse. Jeremiah met with ridicule (verbal abuse), [19] physical abuse (beatings), humiliation (imprisonment first in the stocks at the city gate[20], and later, shut up in 2 different prisons), [21] accusations of treason,[22] abandonment (thrown in a mud cistern and left to die),[23] and many more negative responses which causes great indignity and grief to the heart of both God and his prophet.

Indeed, the governments in Jeremiah's time gave power to individuals deemed worthy by the King to oppress the righteous. Seldom did the king interfere with their activities, no matter how cruel. However, Zedekiah, Israel's last king, showed mercy when a

---

[19] *Jeremiah 18:18*

[20] *Jeremiah 20:2-3*

[21] *Jeremiah 32:2; Jeremiah 33:1*

[22] *Jeremiah 37:13-14*

[23] *Jeremiah 37:15* (house of Jonathan and later house of Malchiah, *Jeremiah 38:6*).

eunuch of the court interceded on behalf of Jeremiah. That king's mercy resulted in Jeremiah's release from a prison of certain death. On another occasion, that same king, Zedekiah, received Jeremiah's pleas not to return to a specific prison house, for that return, again, meant certain death. However, in Judah under these last kings, injustices against both prophet and people raged. While less injustice operated under King Josiah, nevertheless, fairness and equality for all disappeared as a goal for government in the reign of the latter kings of Judah.

JEREMIAH'S SUFFERINGS:

Challenged by the kings, their government, and people, and commanded and inspired by God, Jeremiah continued to declare God's Word, hoping they would heed the call and turn back to God. Sadly, indeed, Judah, as a nation, returned not.

DESCRIPTION OF THEIR STUBBORNNESS:

After much pleading, we hear the Word of YeHoVaH describe their stubbornness:

Jeremiah 6:26-30
"26 O daughter of my people, gird [thee] with sackcloth, and wallow thyself in ashes: make thee mourning, [as for] an only son, most bitter lamentation: for the spoiler shall suddenly come upon

*us. 27 I have set thee [for] a tower [and] a fortress
among my people, that thou mayest know and try their
way. 28 They [are] all grievous revolters, walking
with slanders: [they are] brass and iron; they [are] all
corrupters. 29 The bellows are burned, the lead is
consumed of the fire; the founder melteth in vain: for
the wicked are not plucked away. 30 Reprobate silver
shall [men] call them, because YeHoVaH hath rejected
them. "*

KINGS, NOBLES & GOVERNMENTS FAIL:

In reading Jeremiah, we hear God's call to speak to the
entire nation. God included everyone in the call to
repentance from the king to the nobles which helped
administrate the government, right down to the
private citizen of Judah. Repeatedly, Jeremiah cried
out with passionate pleas to return to God! God and
Jeremiah, too, wanted to spare them what was coming.
Unfortunately, in Jeremiah's time, the government,
who was to set righteous rules, and the leaders to
implement justice, as well as so many others, failed to
follow the plans that God laid out for them. In short,
on every level, they refused to listen.

WHAT ABOUT TODAY:

Truly God's mercy extends to us today, as it did in the
day of Jeremiah. YeHoVaH stills calls everyone born
under heaven to forsake unrighteousness and cling to

the ways of God. YeHoVaH calls to every person living in the land including every form of authority as it stretches from the basest level of authority to the highest government structures in the land.

Governments and their leaders, whether they acknowledge it or not, have a tremendous God-given responsibility to care for the people, and propagate, authorize, and uphold righteous laws and decrees. Scripture verifies that Governments *on every level*, (which includes authorities and leaders from the least to the greatest), all have tremendous responsibility to God! It is no wonder scripture tells us:

1 Timothy 2:1-4
"1 I exhort therefore, that, first of all, supplications, prayers, intercessions, [and] giving of thanks, be made for all men; 2 For kings, and [for] all that are in authority; that we may lead a quiet and peaceable life in all godliness and honesty. 3 For this [is] good and acceptable in the sight of God our Saviour; 4 Who will have all men to be saved, and to come unto the knowledge of the truth. "

Beloved, as a people called of God to obey the Word of God, the precious scriptures, let us ensure we obey this one in Timothy! Let us press into God for our government, all the leaders and the people of the nation! Let us not worry about the political party to whom they belong, nor any personal agendas of leadership. Let us face the Living God and embrace His agenda for He knows the times and seasons in which we live.

In addition, let us do our best to forward evangelism, both through our own mouth and in supporting those ministries who reach out on a larger scale. Let us learn to develop an ear to the Word of God, His take on the society in which we live and how, through prayers, our own obedience to His commands, and the love which YeHoVaH releases to us, see others align their ways with Him, too!

IN REFLECTION:

Jeremiah, no matter the situation, responded with love. YeHoVaH help us to do the same!

MATTERS OF FORSAKEN FAITH

3

"4 Hear ye the word of YeHoVaH, O house of Jacob, and all the families of the house of Israel: 5 Thus saith YeHoVaH, What iniquity have your fathers found in me, that they are gone far from me, and have walked after vanity, and are become vain?"

Jeremiah 2:4-5

Jeremiah opens this Word of YeHoVaH in an address to every living person in Israel. He asks them a point-blank question, which the Almighty placed in his mouth. Paraphrased, the bottom-line states, "Your fathers have gone far from Me, walked after vanity and became vain, but I what have I done to cause it?" Before any answer comes, Jeremiah continues with more statements from YeHoVaH:

Jeremiah 2:6-9
"6 Neither said they, Where [is] YeHoVaH that brought us up out of the land of Egypt, that led us through the wilderness, through a land of deserts and of pits, through a land of drought, and of the shadow of death, through a land that no man passed through, and where no man dwelt? 7 And I brought you into a plentiful country, to eat the fruit thereof and the goodness thereof; but when ye entered, ye defiled my land, and made mine heritage

45

*an abomination. 8 The priests said not, Where [is]
YeHoVaH? and they that handle the law knew me not:
the pastors also transgressed against me, and the
prophets prophesied by Baal, and walked after [things
that] do not profit. 9 Wherefore I will yet plead with
you, saith YeHoVaH, and with your children's children
will I plead. "*

In recapping, YeHoVaH admonishes them for not
seeking Him, the mighty One Who brought them out
of the land of Egypt. He rehearses with them how He
walked their fathers through the dangers of the desert
and brought them into the Promised Land. Upon
entering, they found a plentiful land with much fruit
and goodness. Yet, they defiled that land, and made
His inheritance, which is His People, an abomination[24].

As horrible as that situation is, it gets worse when one
realizes that even the priests, the ones called to serve
the Living God, did not even look for God! They
examined the Torah[25], yet their ardent studies did not
bring them into a knowledge of YeHoVaH, nor
produce a desire to have a relationship with Him! The
pastors, the ones God called to care for His people,
sinned against YeHoVaH, too, as their failed

---

[24] *Deuteronomy 32:9 "For YeHoVaH's portion [is] his people; Jacob [is]
the lot of his inheritance. "*
[25] KJV interprets the word, "Torah" as Law, however, it really
means instructions of God.

understanding of God's Instructions, became the people's portion. To make matters worse, the prophets did not speak YeHoVaH's true word, instead, they prophesied through Baal, a pagan god! The result of such behaviour meant a people robbed of the knowledge of YeHoVaH, and the truth to walk with Him in righteousness and holiness. In addition, none of the precepts which they held as dear led them into a godly and pleasing life before YeHoVaH's Face.

Even still, YeHoVaH pleaded with His People, called by His name, to return to Him. He declared He would continue to cry out to them, at the most for only two more generations, namely that of their children and grandchildren. After that, if God's people did not repent and return to God, He would expel them from their land, and consequently, from His sight. Thus, their continual sinning within the setting of His beloved land, where He led them to live, would end. This unique land, where God intended their light to shine to the nations around them, they would see no more! Darkening that land by sin and their refusal to repent, meant, by God's Mighty Hand, that land would spew them out[26]!

---

[26] Due to God's Mercy, 70 years would pass before their return. In God's order of time, Messiah came, but after that, they'd be scattered to the four corners of the universe!

RELIGION NOT RELATIONSHIP:

In Israel, in many other generations, but especially in this one, the people knew a form of religion, only. Isaiah the prophet, who also prophesied to Judah about her sad state of relationship with God, said:

Isaiah 29:13
> *"13 Wherefore the Lord said, Forasmuch as this people draw near [me] with their mouth, and with their lips do honour me, but have removed their heart far from me, and their fear toward me is taught by the precept of men: "*

These people to whom Isaiah referred, and those to whom Jeremiah addressed, knew how to practice a superficial style "religion", not a deep, endearing fellowship with YeHoVaH.

In Jeremiah's time, as he spoke to God's People, he made it clear that the people had teachers and priests who held in their possessions the oracles of YeHoVaH, yet these voices speaking for the Almighty knew not the Giver of Torah! Instead, they read them, added, and took away from them by their own wisdom, and in doing so, replaced them with idolatrous practices of the land. In effect, they exchanged the truth of YeHoVaH for a lie. This aspect of their life, YeHoVaH longed for them to recognize and from it, flee!

YeHoVaH desired that His people fled from all things that took them away from Him. He longed for them to recognize what was out of sorts, out of alignment with truth, and tossed it out! Then, as they embrace truth, they would walk towards Him. This generation of His People, and those that followed, needed to see Him in the light of their faithful forefathers who remembered Him!

As God's chosen people, they must remember the mighty acts of the One Who, on their behalf, parted the Red Sea, opening a door for them to completely escape a life of slavery to the Pharaoh of Egypt. They needed to rehearse[27] that Red Sea parting, remembering the pursuing Pharaoh and his armies who strove to keep them imprisoned, and once released, to annihilate them when they escaped his grasp.

God's people must see Him in the capacity of the One Who provided for them miraculously feeding them in the desert lands, which they passed through on their journey to the Promised Land. Indeed, they must look to the One Who taught them how to live as a free people, carefully giving them instructions to follow so they may live in true freedom! [28] Such is the promise

---

[27] That rehearsal happens at Passover, as that is a promised feast, or Moedium, (rehearsal) of YeHoVaH.

[28] True freedom is living within the Torah of God, wherein lies the blessings.

of the Torah, which is their key to life within the Promised Land!

If God's people, even in that day as Jeremiah prophesied, returned to YeHoVaH embracing what God gave them, they would live! If not, great trouble and distress heads their way, *arriving soon*. Those events waited on the horizon for the Jeremiah generation, *if* they refused to return to God!

WHAT'S COMING:

In recapping the effects of expressing outward actions to God, but totally missing the heart of the matter, Jeremiah records:

"Jeremiah 14:10
   10 Thus saith YeHoVaH unto this people, Thus have they loved to wander, they have not refrained their feet, therefore YeHoVaH doth not accept them; he will now remember their iniquity, and visit their sins. "

When the heart is not steadfastly secured to the true God, as was in the case with the people to whom Jeremiah prophesied, a wandering away from scripture, its precepts and commands takes place. That wandering leads to a point where hearts no longer restrain their foot from doing evil. Such a heart becomes their own god, their own authority, incorporating whatever seems pleasing to them! With ears tuned to pleasures of the world, philosophies and immediate gratification, these hardened hearts walk in the ways that seem good in their own eyes. They abandon the ways of YeHoVaH, given to produce the best for them.

In modern terms, we might say, "whatever felt good, they did it". Everything they saw which appealed to their flesh, they did. We might sum up their philosophy as "anything goes". In these scenarios, mankind becomes his own judge and jury, totally discarding any possible accountability to the Most High God.

In such a society, truth suffers a fatal wound, and thus, falls in the streets. Mercy becomes the victim of greed![29] In other words, truth is not the source of the common talk of the day. Instead, the conversation centres around the framework of man's own ideas of the good life, based on their own moral code. As this form of society develops, the rich become powerful, making laws for all to obey, but creating loopholes for them! Mercy, if at all meted out, comes in small measures. Its use comes forth *not with the measuring*

---

[29] These statements about truth and mercy, the author heard from the heart of God, as He spoke about the Jeremiah generation and other generations leading up to it!

stick of truth but rather that of money, position, and power. This happens in any society which abandons the basic life instructions of YeHoVaH. This, which we see happening in our world today, happened in ancient Israel. That behaviour escalated the need for Jeremiah's words:

Jeremiah 14: 11-12
> *"11 Then said YeHoVaH unto me, Pray not for this people for [their] good. 12 When they fast, I will not hear their cry; and when they offer burnt offering and an oblation, I will not accept them: but I will consume them by the sword, and by the famine, and by the pestilence. "*

YeHoVaH, thoroughly distressed with His People's treatment of Him as their God, says, "Don't pray for this people for their good". Why? They cannot receive good or else they will see it as a reward for their behaviour and keep on doing what they are doing to their own detriment.   YeHoVaH continues, "When they fast, I won't hear their cry. Their burnt offerings and oblations I will not see as acceptable." Why? Their heart was not in it! These possessed the heart of a performance-style religious person.   Their worship activities, spurred on by reason of outward performance, unaffected God's heart.   He looked inside to the emptiness of their heart!

Then, YeHoVaH issued His righteous decree upon this perverse, lying, wicked and pretentious generation: *"but I will consume them by the sword, and by the famine, and by the pestilence"*. This generation, due to their wickedness and refusal to repent, stands ready to experience war, hunger, epidemics, and the like. This generation, unworthy to receive good from the Almighty, awaits their just dues.

Jeremiah 14:13
"13 Then said I, Ah, Lord GOD! behold, the prophets say unto them, Ye shall not see the sword, neither shall ye have famine; but I will give you assured peace in this place. "

Here is where the false prophets of their day take their toll! They look at the circumstances, but due to their inability to grasp the true counsel of the Almighty decree only good things will happen. They say, "No! You will not have war or go hungry! No, I assure you, you are going to have peace!". Thus, the people's hearts turn even further away from the true God, believing their life, which they think is good, produces good. They erase accountability to God with logic, bombastic rhetoric, political or personal agendas of false prophets, who wish to receive accolades and approval among the people of the land. They tell them what they want to hear, not what God's Word decrees!

YeHoVaH, then, speaks of these prophets, wrapped up in religious ideals, experiencing false dreams and visions:

Jeremiah 14:14-16
> *"14 Then YeHoVaH said unto me, The prophets prophesy lies in my name: I sent them not, neither have I commanded them, neither spake unto them: they prophesy unto you a false vision and divination, and a thing of nought, and the deceit of their heart. 15 Therefore thus saith YeHoVaH concerning the prophets that prophesy in my name, and I sent them not, yet they say, Sword and famine shall not be in this land; By sword and famine shall those prophets be consumed. 16 And the people to whom they prophesy shall be cast out in the streets of Jerusalem because of the famine and the sword; and they shall have none to bury them, them, their wives, nor their sons, nor their daughters: for I will pour their wickedness upon them. "*

YeHoVaH makes it clear: the prophets prophesy lies in My name; I did not send them; I did not command them to go; I did not speak to them.

These prophets, whose words refuse alignment with God's word and His heart for His People, speak false visions and those of divination. They speak from the deceitfulness of their own hearts, for they do not see the light of the truth!

YeHoVaH, however, gives a pronouncement of their fate. Since they said the sword (war) and famine (hunger, crop failure, embargos on food, etc.) will not come, it shall come and consume these prophets. Now, both false prophet and adherents to their doctrine, will find themselves tossed into the streets experiencing the sword and famine. No one shall bury them nor their loved ones when they die. None will mourn them! Their loss on this earth passes without notice.

Jeremiah, YeHoVaH commands, weep night and day. Cry without ceasing, for the virgin daughter of my people, (the one with such a promising future) is broken with a great breach. Yes, she is in great distress, having been dealt a grievous blow. See this and weep!

Dear Reader, this is the horrible end of an outward form of religion that goes on generation after generation, abandoning the One Who alone can save them. Yes, this is the end of an empty and vain religion with only an outside form of worship, with nothing rooted in the heart. This is the end of the people when the leaders, who are to teach them truth and lead them in it, know not the truth and in their own vanities, teach their own ideals and values to listening ears. This is the end of such manmade rules and practices which foster corruption, immorality, and even depravity amongst the living. This is the end of the ones who seek to live their own life, make themselves their own god, to whom they make themselves accountable!

Make no mistake, people of such form and stature drastically affect the entire society in which they live as they propagate followers. Their erroneous behaviour works through their society like leaven does through dough. In the end, such a society moves far away from the true God, the One Who created the heavens and the earth and set the foundations of the earth in place. This is a horrible, and heart-breaking end of any people, society, or nation, but especially catastrophic for those *who once knew God* and abandoned Him for other gods or other things!

Dear one, as you read this book and study this course, if YeHoVaH presents your society or nation to you like this, then weep and cry, like Jeremiah, without ceasing until God reassures you things will change. Keep in mind, too, if you live in a nation with Judeo-Christian roots, that sad state happened as a direct result of *the people of God*, gradually abandoning their responsibility to know and obey Him. When any society arrives at such a horrific state, dear one, do not blame that society! It is but the result of the body of Messiah, (believers of the ekklesia[30]) forsaking Him, rejecting His cry to return and repent!

If your spiritual vision perceives this as such, cry aloud to God from the depth of your being. Shout to God with groaning and languishing to spare your generation! YeHoVaH's heart, moved with pity for such a state, is well able to revive His people who have forsaken Him, and in His Mercy make them an impetus for change in their society within the very nation in which they live.

Dear faithful one, press into heaven until you have your answer! Even if you perceive revival in your midst, press in more and more until you see a difference, until every one that lives in ear shot of your voice receives a word, a touch, or an action from the Hand of the Almighty! Indeed, dear reader, do this and realize that this is the cry of the true people of God who possess hope to change the world around them! This is the cry of the Jeremiah generation!

---

[30] church

MATTERS OF
HARDENED HEARTS

4

"Thus saith YeHoVaH; Cursed [be] the man that trusteth in man, and maketh flesh his arm, and whose heart departeth from YeHoVaH.

Jeremiah 17:5

While kings, nobles and priests heard, then rejected and dismissed the words of Jeremiah, the prophet, God had a further admonition to the common people. These people, although uninvolved in the running of the governmental systems, nevertheless, needed exposure to God's response to injustice. Most of them, although living within the parameters of poverty, like people of all walks of life, made choices that affected others. If they took the behaviour of these elite members of society as examples on how to live, then, they too, need to repent and get right with God. On that note, explaining the problem in front of them, Jeremiah related the following:

Jeremiah 17:1-10
  "1 The sin of Judah [is] written with a pen of iron, [and] with the point of a diamond: [it is] graven upon the table of their heart, and upon the horns of your altars;

2 Whilst their children remember their altars and their groves by the green trees upon the high hills. 3 O my mountain in the field, I will give thy substance [and] all thy treasures to the spoil, [and] thy high places for sin, throughout all thy borders. 4 And thou, even thyself, shalt discontinue from thine heritage that I gave thee; and I will cause thee to serve thine enemies in the land which thou knowest not: for ye have kindled a fire in mine anger, [which] shall burn for ever.

5 Thus saith YeHoVaH; Cursed [be] the man that trusteth in man, and maketh flesh his arm, and whose heart departeth from YeHoVaH. 6 For he shall be like the heath in the desert, and shall not see when good cometh; but shall inhabit the parched places in the wilderness, [in] a salt land and not inhabited. 7 Blessed [is] the man that trusteth in YeHoVaH, and whose hope YeHoVaH is.

8 For he shall be as a tree planted by the waters, and [that] spreadeth out her roots by the river, and shall not see when heat cometh, but her leaf shall be green; and shall not be careful in the year of drought, neither shall cease from yielding fruit. 9 The heart [is] deceitful above all [things], and desperately wicked: who can know it? 10 I YeHoVaH search the heart, [I] try the reins, even to give every man according to his ways, [and] according to the fruit of his doings. "

This address, which Jeremiah gave, not only included the common people, but it defined the root of the problem. They became so one with their sin, it was etched like carvings, deeply imbedded upon their hearts. YeHoVaH compared it to the etchings they carved on the horns of their altars! What was their sin, what was that practice which they performed and passed on to their children?

From Jeremiah's discourse and what we know of their religious practices at that time, part of their practices included sacrificing their children to Molech in the valley of Tophet.

> *Jeremiah 7:31*
> *"31 And they have built the high places of Tophet, which [is] in the valley of the son of Hinnom, to burn their sons and their daughters in the fire; which I commanded [them] not, neither came it into my heart. "*

These people to whom Jeremiah addressed, embraced this abominable practice of killing their children under the falsehood of worship to God. YeHoVaH hated this thing, as well as the other practices Israel incorporated as worship to YeHoVaH. As a direct result of their pagan ceremonies, which they did for their own pleasure or desire for reward, He promised to ruin. All the fruits of their labours, their substance, their treasures the spoiler would take. All their altars in high places where they sinned against God, the plunderer would cast down and destroy. Their treasured religious rites, which YeHoVaH did not order, nor even allowed the thought to enter His mind, He declared eliminated.

No longer would God look on their sin which they would not forsake. If they would not remove it voluntarily, YeHoVaH would do it for them. All throughout the borders of Israel their abominable practices would cease because they would not live there to practice them when God's hand of Judgment came down:

Jeremiah 15:2
"2 And it shall come to pass, if they say unto thee, Whither shall we go forth? then thou shalt tell them, Thus saith YeHoVaH; Such as [are] for death, to death; and such as [are] for the sword, to the sword; and such as [are] for the famine, to the famine; and such as [are] for the captivity, to the captivity. "

When God's hand of punishment finally came, some died, some experienced great distress, some went hungry, some became captives. YeHoVaH promised that by His Hand, His heritage would be gone! No longer His People, they became fodder for their enemies and served them in a strange land called Babylon.

Yes, all this came upon them because they kindled a fire in God's heart which could not be quenched! This was the result of their choices as they rejected His call for repentance, stubbornly refused to release their wicked ways and by their behaviour denied God as their Father. They totally refused to align with God's call to embrace Him, did not acknowledge Him as the Holy One of Israel, desiring to fulfill the purpose of God for them. God created them a holy people and they became an abomination before His Eyes. Defy the Master's Hand, refuse to repent, live as you desire, adopt, and practice unrestrained evil **and** still call yourself My People! Do this and this is what awaits you, says YeHoVaH!

Jeremiah 17:5-6
 "5   Thus saith YeHoVaH; Cursed [be] the man that trusteth in man, and maketh flesh his arm, and whose heart departeth from YeHoVaH. 6 For he shall be like the heath in the desert, and shall not see when good cometh; but shall inhabit the parched places in the wilderness, [in] a salt land and not inhabited.

A CONTRAST:

In contrast to the above behaviour, Jeremiah adds,

Jeremiah 17:7-8

> *"7 Blessed [is] the man that trusteth in YeHoVaH, and whose hope YeHoVaH is. 8 For he shall be as a tree planted by the waters, and [that] spreadeth out her roots by the river, and shall not see when heat cometh, but her leaf shall be green; and shall not be careful in the year of drought, neither shall cease from yielding fruit".*

Answers to such behaviour as Jeremiah addressed, lies in the advice of scripture:

Proverbs 4:4

> *"4 He taught me also, and said unto me, Let thine heart retain my words: keep my commandments, and live. "*

Proverbs 7:2

> *"2 Keep my commandments, and live; and my law as the apple of thine eye. "*

Proverbs 9:6

> *"6 Forsake the foolish, and live; and go in the way of understanding. "*

Here lies the way of life! YeHoVaH desired they take that way! Why did they refuse? What was the root of their inability to change? Jeremiah addresses it:

Jeremiah 17:9-10

"9 The heart [is] deceitful above all [things], and desperately wicked: who can know it? 10 I YeHoVaH search the heart, [I] try the reins, even to give every man according to his ways, [and] according to the fruit of his doings. "

Earlier, Jeremiah spoke of their hearts engraved with sin, for they became so one with it, it became part of them.

Here, Jeremiah explains the root of the problem is not God's inability to communicate with them. Influences such as upbringing, teaching and peer pressure can add to the problem, but the root of the problem is the heart! It is deceitful above all things! It tricks one into thinking they are doing well, they are good, doing right; they are good with God!

That human heart, that very throne from where choices rule, God calls desperately wicked! In fact, Jeremiah declares, "Who can know it?" In short, no one knows their own heart, nor the depth of it, nor the motives within! However, God knows it and He searches the heart.

Here, then, lies the solution to the heart's problem! Come before YeHoVaH and ask Him to search it!

Jeremiah 17:10
> "10 I YeHoVaH search the heart, [I] try the reins, even
> to give every man according to his ways, [and]
> according to the fruit of his doings. "

A TIMELESS SOLUTION:

This was their solution as presented to them in the time
of Jeremiah. *Unfortunately, they did not accept it.*
They did not reach beyond their own understanding,
nor seek God to help them do so. Instead, the horrible,
promised judgment came to them. They experienced
great distress beyond words to describe. Many
experienced starvation, brutal slavery and a great
many died violently by the sword.

*****

Dear Reader, please take this lesson to heart! Remember this admonition:

Hebrews 4:7b
  "7 b) To day if ye will hear his voice, harden not your hearts".

No matter where you are with God, dear one, please take some time on this topic and bring it before Him. Invite Him to examine the very depths of your being, you know, those deep and secret things in your heart. Ask Him to investigate, thoroughly into every nook and cranny! Ask Him to probe deep until He sees His own heart looking back at Him!

Our hearts do matter as it determines the choices of our everyday life, in the here and now, which affects our eternal rewards when this life ends. In short, the heart matters greatly!

MATTERS OF
ALTERED AUTHORITY

5

"13 O YeHoVaH the hope of Israel, all that forsake thee shall be ashamed, [and] they that depart from me shall be written in the earth, because they have forsaken YeHoVaH, the fountain of living waters.   14 Heal me, O YeHoVaH and I shall be healed; save me, and I shall be saved: for thou [art] my praise. "

Jeremiah 17:13-14

I srael departed from YeHoVaH, and in doing so, they forsook Him.   Thus, the memory of their existence upon the earth shall be as transient as dust blown in the wind. Different to the names of His faithful servants, who God writes in the book of life,[31] these children of Israel to whom God addressed, shall find no honour, no lasting memory for good upon the earth.   Such is the plight of the ones who refuse to return to God!

Throughout the book of Jeremiah, we hear the prophet's cries to the people to repent, to turn away from that which kept them from YeHoVaH. Jeremiah echoes God's heart as he speaks against their offensive behaviour before God.   His words fell upon ears that

---

[31] *Malachi 3:16*

would not hear! Jeremiah, expressing God's grief in the matter declares:

Jeremiah 9:1-3
> *"1 Oh that my head were waters, and mine eyes a fountain of tears, that I might weep day and night for the slain of the daughter of my people! 2 Oh that I had in the wilderness a lodging place of wayfaring men; that I might leave my people, and go from them! for they be all adulterers, an assembly of treacherous men.*
> *3 And they bend their tongues like their bow for lies: but they are not valiant for the truth upon the earth; for they proceed from evil to evil, and they know not me, saith YeHoVaH. "*

Jeremiah describes the people as "adulterers, an assembly of treacherous men". He defines them as "not valiant for the truth upon the earth". He depicts their behaviour saying, "they proceed from evil to evil". Then, Jeremiah, with emphasis, points out the bottom line, stating they abandoned Him, for indeed, says YeHoVaH, "They know Me!"

Jeremiah 9:4-8
> *"4 Take ye heed every one of his neighbour, and trust ye not in any brother: for every brother will utterly supplant, and every neighbour will walk with slanders.*
> *5 And they will deceive every one his neighbour, and will not speak the truth: they have taught their tongue*

to speak lies, [and] weary themselves to commit iniquity.

6 Thine habitation [is] in the midst of deceit; through deceit they refuse to know me, saith YeHoVaH. 7 Therefore thus saith YeHoVaH of hosts, Behold, I will melt them, and try them; for how shall I do for the daughter of my people? 8 Their tongue [is as] an arrow shot out; it speaketh deceit: [one] speaketh peaceably to his neighbour with his mouth, but in heart he layeth his wait. "

In Israel at that time, their social behaviour, so demoralized and degenerate, expressed itself by slandering their neighbours, speaking lies against them, and also betraying their own brothers (family). One neighbour deceives another, betrays them, not speaking the truth because they trained their tongue to lies! So often did these sins transpire that they became tired from committing their iniquities. Jeremiah declares that even in the very place where they dwelt, imprisoned by the grasp of deceit, when the strain of their sins increased, they refused to abandon their ways and cry out to YeHoVaH. They rejected His call to know Him!

Furthermore, their tongue is like an arrow shot out from a bow speaking only deceit. He speaks peace to his neighbour to disarm him, but in his heart, he waits to get the upper hand on the neighbour to take control of his goods, property, or treasures. Somehow these deceitful people strove to benefit from that neighbour's downfall as the neighbour fell into the trap, the very one they set for them.

Jeremiah 11:9-10
"9 And YeHoVaH said unto me, A conspiracy is found among the men of Judah, and among the inhabitants of Jerusalem. 10 They are turned back to the iniquities of their forefathers, which refused to hear my words; and they went after other gods to serve them: the house of Israel and the house of Judah have broken my covenant which I made with their fathers. "

Plans such as lying, defamation of character, traps to catch their neighbour to destroy them freely operated, giving conspiracy a home. If that did not seem bad enough, they turned their backs to the One Who redeemed them! They went back to the idolatrous behaviour of their forefathers who refused to hear the words of correction that YeHoVaH spoke to them. They went to other gods and served them! Summarizing it in one statement, "they broke the covenant which YeHoVaH made with their fathers". With such a covenant broken, what remained?

Their loyalty to God became a victim of idolatry. Their integrity to watch over their neighbour to benefit the neighbour turned to spying out their property to add to their own greed. Their iniquities, so intense in practice, hardened their hearts to the point of refusal to hear the Word of YeHoVaH, through the mouth of His true prophets.

Instead, the people flocked to false prophets who reinforced their sin, for these prophets lived in sin themselves:

Jeremiah 23:14
"14 I have seen also in the prophets of Jerusalem an horrible thing: they commit adultery, and walk in lies: they strengthen also the hands of evildoers, that none doth return from his wickedness: they are all of them unto me as Sodom, and the inhabitants thereof as Gomorrah. "

Prophets, who walk with the true and living God, call the people back to a life pleasing to YeHoVaH. They identify sin, they point out ways that offend the Living God in the hopes their listeners see it God's way, repent and return to God. False prophets, on the other hand, reinforce the sin of their followers, while they, too, lie and commit adultery.

YeHoVaH addressed this directly:

Jeremiah 11:7-8
"7 For I earnestly protested unto your fathers in the day [that] I brought them up out of the land of Egypt,

73

[even] unto this day, rising early and protesting, saying, Obey my voice. 8 Yet they obeyed not, nor inclined their ear, but walked every one in the imagination of their evil heart: therefore I will bring upon them all the words of this covenant, which I commanded [them] to do; but they did [them] not. "

Because none obeyed His voice, none valued truth above lies, YeHoVaH promised to bring the curses of the covenant upon them. Indeed, walking after the imagination of their heart, going from sin to sin, refusing to hear the true word of YeHoVaH, they would receive the recompense of doing things their way.

Isaiah summarizes this type of life in his message to Israel:

Isaiah 5:18-24
> *"18 Woe unto them that draw iniquity with cords of vanity, and sin as it were with a cart rope: 19 That say, Let him make speed, [and] hasten his work, that we may see [it]: and let the counsel of the Holy One of Israel draw nigh and come, that we may know [it]! 20 Woe unto them that call evil good, and good evil; that put darkness for light, and light for darkness; that put bitter for sweet, and sweet for bitter! 21 Woe unto [them that are] wise in their own eyes, and prudent in their own sight! 22 Woe unto [them that are] mighty to drink wine, and men of strength to mingle strong drink: 23 Which justify*

the wicked for reward, and take away the righteousness of the righteous from him! 24 Therefore as the fire devoureth the stubble, and the flame consumeth the chaff, [so] their root shall be as rottenness, and their blossom shall go up as dust: because they have cast away the law of YeHoVaH of hosts, and despised the word of the Holy One of Israel. "

WHY WANT TRUTH?

Isaiah 5:1 -24 (the above scripture) recaps the end of sin. God's viewpoint, so different than mankind's, presents sin as a web of iniquity spun for those who come into agreement with its clinging appeal:

- Sorrow, trouble, indignation, and distress[32] comes to those who draw or bring to themselves iniquity, pulling it with cords of vanity (or pride). They draw sin towards themselves, in the same manner as one who pulls on a rope attached to a cart, drawing the cart near to them.
- They challenge God to perform His promised destructions quickly. They sarcastically invite His Counsel to draw near so they can see if it works for them.
- Their version of truth stands in misalignment as they see good as evil and evil as good. They embrace what lies in the darkness and reject what lives in the light. They call bitter things

---

[32] These are all words to define "woe".

75

(that of darkness) sweet and sweet things (that
of God) bitter.

- They view their own wisdom as wiser than
  God, and in their own eyes, see their choices as
  sensible, when in fact it is contrary to God's
  ideals for them.
- They get their strength from strong drink rather
  than repenting and turning to God to sustain
  them in their troubles.
- They justify the wicked by making excuses for
  them, often in exchange for personal gain or
  reward. They take away the righteousness of
  the righteous! In other words, they try to make
  the righteous look evil.[33]

This behaviour, reaching its climax or fullest
expression, invites the fire of God's fury. Like flames
quickly eat up the chaff, so their root swiftly becomes
rotten, and their flower, which they struggled to
produce, becomes like dust. In short, their life holds
no fruit and their rewards total none! This ending
awaits all who toss out the Law of YeHoVaH Tseva'ot
and despise the Word of the Holy One of Israel.

---

[33] *An example* in Jeremiah days: Jeremiah calls child sacrifice an
abomination. Those performing the rite claim differently and as
Jeremiah points the finger at them, they point it back at him,
accusing him. Jeremiah's righteous stance, in their mind, makes
Jeremiah the villain.

AN ABSENCE OF TRUTH COSTS:

Putting it in the simplest form possible, God, His Word, His Promises, His Laws and Statutes lead mankind to truth. They pave a way of life which is righteous, promises true favour with God in the here and now and in eternity.

On the opposite spectrum, refusing to listen, blatantly disobeying, making one's own laws, or embracing lifestyles contrary to God's Biblical admonitions means a life of trouble. Without repentance, it leads to eternal death. Those who follow the latter, hold hands with the Anti-Christ and his system.

Paul's letter to Timothy addresses the Anti-Christ spirit and gives the bottom line for those who choose the Anti-Christ lifestyle:

2 Thessalonians 2:9-12
 "9 [Even him], whose coming is after the working of Satan with all power and signs and lying wonders, 10 And with all deceivableness of unrighteousness in them that perish; because they received not the love of the truth, that they might be saved. 11 And for this cause God shall send them strong delusion, that they should believe a lie: 12 That they all might be damned who believed not the truth, but had pleasure in unrighteousness. "

77

WHAT IS THE BOTTOM LINE?

Verse 10 states, "they received not the love of the truth". Had Israel received that "love of the truth", they would recognize it and accept it in its presented form, namely, in God's Word, His Promises, His Laws and Statutes. They would then forsake all that stands contrary. They would, instead, align with truth!

THE ROOTS OF INJUSTICE:

In summary, the people, from the richest, most powerful down to the poorest, weakest member of that society failed to receive the truth. Instead, they loved their sin! They rejected the idea of repentance and continued following their own way.

Things degraded, and as it did, injustices flourished even more as they walked away from the Laws of God, the worship of the Holy One of Israel and instead, embraced many idolatrous practices of the pagan world around them. They lost their separation from evil! Embracing evil, they became one with it.

Those deep roots of injustice, from which they refused to repent, spread like a wild vine into every aspect of life within the nation. Their pagan ideals, which spoke loudly against the truth of YeHoVaH, spread its tentacles into every aspect of life. It became the foundation for the operation of the nation moving away from God's prescribed order. Authority moved from the scripture (Torah or God's instructions) to the king to his courts, to the nobles, to the wealthy landowners, and then to the family units who did the bulk of the work for the nation, often in slavery.

Prosperity's goal flipped their God-ordained society, and so much so that the ones with the greatest treasures ruled, under the lineage of a descendant of King David. Instead of God's authority first, His Laws and commandments, upheld by kings and priests and rulers of integrity in the land, they installed their own laws, oppressed the poor, the broken, the widow, and the orphan. In other words, instead of following the biblical outline as God designed it, they operated against the grain of the Godly structure of the universe and for that, they paid dearly!

LESSONS FROM ISRAEL'S SITUATION:

Dear reader, the injustice in the society where Jeremiah prophesied, began to decline bit by bit, one generation at a time. It began by a digression away from an established righteous law, practice, or truth, which became victim of persuasive lies.

In short, righteousness met with sin, and sin took it captive! Deductive reason took over the commands of scripture, removing the bar of holiness from their lifestyle.

In recapping the injustices taking place prior to and during the time of Jeremiah's prophesy, we see idolatry, greed, hatred, slander or swearing falsely for money, position, and power. We hear of murder of the innocent babies in sacrifice to Molech, coveting of neighbours' lifestyle, family, and possessions. We hear of slavery, oppression of the sick, the needy, the widow and the orphan. We see people declaring their own values and ideals above the Word of God, claiming equal authority with God to bring their manmade laws into existence.

In short, we see people doing whatever seemed right in their own eyes and doing it all for personal gain! We see a generation self-focused, forsaking all forms of righteousness and truth, making up rules as they go along. Into this scene, YeHoVaH sent Jeremiah to call His People to repent and return to Him! In the next section, you will look at how Jeremiah became God's voice, accepted his call and then, poured out his life for the return of the people to God.

You will have opportunity to mark in your mind and heart the character of the prophet Jeremiah. As you do, look for his strengths and weaknesses. See how he handled both! Look for his ability to stand in the hour in which he lived and the tools he incorporated to come out of the fire unscathed! Look at Jeremiah and see what God requires to send His Voice to a "Jeremiah Generation".

COURSE 801

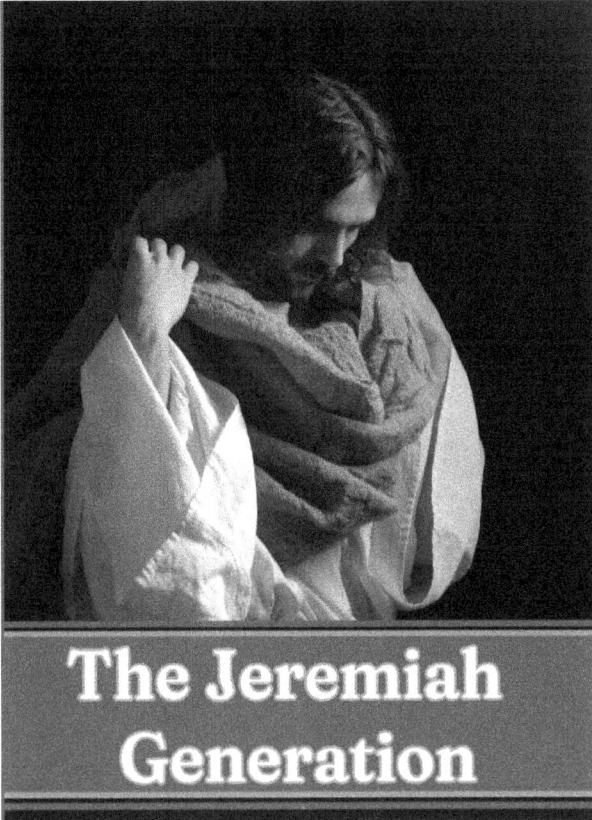

The Jeremiah Generation

SECTION 2:

INJUSTICE REFUTED

(Prophet & Powerful Message)

MATTERS OF PRIESTLY PARENTAGE

6

"I have sent also unto you all my servants the prophets, rising up early[34] and sending them, saying, Return ye now every man from his evil way, and amend your doings, and go not after other gods to serve them, and ye shall dwell in the land which I have given to you and to your fathers: but ye have not inclined your ear, nor hearkened unto me. "

Jeremiah 35:15

YeHoVaH, desires all people to know Him. Once their words lay claim to the fact that they belong to Him, YeHoVaH desires they look like, act like, speak like, think, and respond like He does! For this transformation to take place in the lives of adherents to faith in Him, YeHoVaH helps His people in many ways, including an empowerment to obey, and most importantly, He instructs them well. His words of instructions, found in the Torah, provide directives to living a life pleasing in His sight and exemplifying His character.

---

[34] This phrase, "rising up early", Jeremiah used 6 times throughout the book: *Jeremiah 7:13 Jeremiah 7:25 Jeremiah 26:5; Jeremiah 29:19 Jeremiah 32:33; Jeremiah 35:15*

Unfortunately, especially under the First Covenant, not everyone understands those instructions. Therefore, God installed the office of teacher.

Under the First Covenant, each father taught his family how to obey the Torah. They learned it from two sources: their forefathers and the priests of God, whose job incorporated educating the people to know YeHoVaH and follow His commands and precepts. Of this office, YeHoVaH spoke:

Malachi 2:7
"7 For the priest's lips should keep knowledge, and they should seek the law at his mouth: for he [is] the messenger of YeHoVaH of hosts. "

While this scripture comes from a time after Jeremiah, its message gives reference to a well-known truth. It shows us a standard focal point on how God perceived the priesthood. Let us look at that passage within its setting:

Malachi 2:4-7
"4 And ye shall know that I have sent this commandment unto you, that my covenant might be with Levi, saith YeHoVaH of hosts. 5 My covenant was with him of life and peace; and I gave them to him [for] the fear wherewith he feared me, and was afraid before my name. 6 The law of truth was in his mouth, and iniquity was not found in his lips: he walked with

me in peace and equity, and did turn many away from
iniquity. 7 For the priest's lips should keep knowledge,
and they should seek the law at his mouth: for he [is]
the messenger of YeHoVaH of hosts. "

God's people, those who desired to know the truth, should seek the priest's of YeHoVaH to teach them truth. Of this, God spoke clearly. He inaugurated the priesthood for many reasons, including relating truth to His People.

People, then, from Moses and the giving of the Law, onward, knew that teaching of the Word, mandated by God for all to know, must come from the lips of the priests. Thus, making the priestly lineage of Levi,[35] amongst their other duties, responsible to know YeHoVaH and His Word, communicating it correctly to God's people. With the importance of this line of Levi in mind, let us look at Jeremiah's lineage.

Jeremiah 1:1
   "1 The words of Jeremiah the son of Hilkiah, of the
   priests that [were] in Anathoth in the land of
   Benjamin[36]:"

---

[35] Levi's father was Aaron, the brother of Moses.

[36] This does not mean that Jeremiah was a Benjamite. It is merely the piece of land where the Levites lived.

This passage, which opens the book of Jeremiah, clearly states that Jeremiah's lineage is that of the priests.[37] His father, Hilkiah and his lineage, scripture does not relate in this passage, however, many believe Jeremiah's father was the High priest Hilkiah, as referred to in *2 Kings 22 and 2 Chronicles 34*. This high priest Hilkiah ministered at the time of Josiah, and five years into the prophetic ministry of Jeremiah, found the book of the Law in the house of YeHoVaH[38].

Nevertheless, Jeremiah's lineage was Levitical and therefore, he had a mandate to teach the people. As a priest, he would enter the service of YeHoVaH at the age of 25:

Numbers 8:23-26

"23 And YeHoVaH spake unto Moses, saying, 24 This [is it] that [belongeth] unto the Levites: from twenty and five years old and upward they shall go in to wait upon the service of the tabernacle of the congregation: 25 And from the age of fifty years they shall cease waiting upon the service [thereof], and shall serve no more: 26 But shall minister with their brethren in the tabernacle of the congregation, to keep the charge, and

---

[37] Jeremiah lived in Judah, and unlike the lineage of priesthood of the Northern Israelites which Jeroboam changed, Judah's priesthood remained centred in Levi.

[38] Jews believe Jeremiah, indeed, was the son of Hilkiah, the High Priest. "Jeremiah was born of a priestly family, in the town of Anathoth in Benjamin. His father was the prophet and High Priest Hilkiah. "

shall do no service. Thus shalt thou do unto the Levites touching their charge. "

YeHoVaH, however, had a different plan for Jeremiah. We see this as Jeremiah gives us a clue to his approximate age when YeHoVaH called him as a prophet:

Jeremiah 1:4-10
"4 Then the word of YeHoVaH came unto me, saying, 5 Before I formed thee in the belly I knew thee; and before thou camest forth out of the womb I sanctified thee, [and] I ordained thee a prophet unto the nations. 6 Then said I, Ah, Lord GOD! behold, I cannot speak: for I [am] a child.

7 But YeHoVaH said unto me, Say not, I [am] a child: for thou shalt go to all that I shall send thee, and whatsoever I command thee thou shalt speak. 8 Be not afraid of their faces: for I [am] with thee to deliver thee, saith YeHoVaH. 9 Then YeHoVaH put forth his hand, and touched my mouth. And YeHoVaH said unto me, Behold, I have put my words in thy mouth. 10 See, I have this day set thee over the nations and over the kingdoms, to root out, and to pull down, and to destroy, and to throw down, to build, and to plant. "

In verse 6, Jeremiah says, *"Then said I, Ah, Lord GOD! Behold, I cannot speak: for I [am] a child."*

In Hebrew, the word נַעַר (nah'-ar) means a young man, a child, a lad, a youth[39]. According to Jewish tradition, a child becomes a man when he is responsible for his own choices, including his own Jewish learning. At age 13, a Jewish boy enjoys marking his teenage years with a Bar Mitzvah, which declares he is now a man. That ancient tradition of the Jews makes it quite possible that Jeremiah was not yet 13.[40]

At whatever age YeHoVaH called Jeremiah, we know God gave Jeremiah some clear qualities to understand:

- Jeremiah must go to all those to whom God sends him and he must speak whatever God commands him to say. (vs 7)
- Jeremiah's conduct must focus on God's presence with him; thus, he should not be afraid for God will deliver him. (vs 8)
- Jeremiah must know that YeHoVaH put His words into Jeremiah's mouth. (vs 9)
- Jeremiah, as God commanded, must remember that God set him over nations and over the kingdoms. (vs 10)

---

[39] Strong's Concordance Hebrew Word # 5288.
[40] Others say he was around the age of 17, while still others say older.

- Jeremiah's ministry included rooting out, pulling down, destroying, and throwing down the unrighteous strongholds which lay embedded within the nation. After these things leave, then comes building and planting. (vs 10)

Verse 10 clearly indicates Jeremiah's task from the Almighty, including confrontations to those who held dear to their present religious practices. Consequently, confronting them with their behavioural offences against God could only meet with resistance, for this was a stubborn, hard hearted people! We see this early within the Word of YeHoVaH to Jeremiah in Chapter 1:

Jeremiah 1:14-19
"14 Then YeHoVaH said unto me, Out of the north an evil shall break forth upon all the inhabitants of the land. 15 For, lo, I will call all the families of the kingdoms of the north, saith YeHoVaH; and they shall come, and they shall set every one his throne at the entering of the gates of Jerusalem, and against all the walls thereof round about, and against all the cities of Judah. 16 And I will utter my judgments against them touching all their wickedness, who have forsaken me, and have burned incense unto other gods, and worshipped the works of their own hands.

17 Thou therefore gird up thy loins, and arise, and speak unto them all that I command thee: be not dismayed at their faces, lest I confound thee before them. 18 For, behold, I have made thee this day a defenced city, and an iron pillar, and brasen walls against the whole land, against the kings of Judah, against the princes thereof, against the priests thereof, and against the people of the land. 19 And they shall fight against thee; but they shall not prevail against thee; for I [am] with thee, saith YeHoVaH, to deliver thee. "

Recapping these verses, we see that 14 to 15 relate specifics of a Judgment coming. Verse 16 describes the why:

- Out of the North evil breaks forth on this land. (vs 14)
- The thrones[41] of the North come at the entrance of the gates of Jerusalem, and besiege it, and all the cities of Judah. (vs 15)
- I will utter my judgments against them touching all their wickedness: (vs 16)
  - They have forsaken me.
  - They have burned incense unto other gods.
  - They have worshipped the works of their own hands.

---

[41] Thrones, which suggest authority, rulership, government, here represents Nebuchadnezzar's Government

Verse 17 to 19 describes the people's attitude, as well as how Jeremiah should think:

- Prepare yourself to face them, Jeremiah! (Gird up your loins!) Arise, and speak unto them all that I command thee. Do not let their faces deter you from giving them the message which I put in your mouth! (vs 17)
- Know that you are strong and protected! ("I have made you a defenced city, and an iron pillar, and brazen walls against the whole land, against the kings of Judah, against the princes thereof, against the priests thereof, and against the people of the land"). (vs 18)
- They will fight against you, Jeremiah, but they will not win because I am with you to deliver you. (vs 19)

Jeremiah, no matter his age, must open his mouth and speak the exact words God implanted. He could not look at the faces of those to whom he spoke, analyzing their response either in support or rejection of his words. Looking at his audience must not be his measuring stick! He must keep his eyes on God and what he received from Him.

Jeremiah must remember, too, that his words, once spoken, will produce problems. Those who heard his words will not like what he said! They will not perceive that the words, which challenge their practices, align with truth. They will not classify Jeremiah as speaking for YeHoVaH because his words will not align with what they deemed as correct! Jeremiah will not win their approval. These people will fight against Jeremiah to prove him wrong and overthrow any influence which may arise. Except for a few individuals, Jeremiah, either in his own person or in his role as a prophet, cannot expect to be accepted amongst his people[42].

For the prophet Jeremiah, these words of Yeshua truly apply:

Luke 6:22-23
> *"22 Blessed are ye, when men shall hate you, and when they shall separate you [from their company], and shall reproach [you], and cast out your name as evil, for the Son of man's sake. 23 Rejoice ye in that day, and leap for joy: for, behold, your reward [is] great in heaven: for in the like manner did their fathers unto the prophets. "*

Jeremiah, a true prophet of God, *like Yeshua and His true followers,* experienced the negative reaction of crowds. In Israel, during Jeremiah's time, inhabitants of the land which offended the living God, preferred to keep

---

[42] Is it any wonder biblical history calls Jeremiah the Weeping Prophet!

their sins than to repent![43] God, however, perceived the situation differently, and so must His prophet! Jeremiah, the chosen vessel of YeHoVaH, must prepare himself for what lay ahead. Jeremiah met more than objection, more than rejection. As Jeremiah preached the Word of God, he experienced persecution, imprisonment and more!

Nevertheless, YeHoVaH wanted the people of God to repent. Thus, long before the actual judgments began to fall, He equipped and sent Jeremiah to confront them. He did so "rising up early", as Jeremiah declared six times in the book of Jeremiah:

Jeremiah 35:15
   "I have sent also unto you all my servants the prophets, **rising up early** *and sending them, saying, Return ye now every man from his evil way, and amend your doings, and go not after other gods to serve them, and ye shall dwell in the land which I have given to you and to your fathers: but ye have not inclined your ear, nor hearkened unto me. "*

---

[43] Such resistance still awaits those today, who speak the word of YeHoVaH to those who prefer to keep their own practices, no matter whom they offend!

MATTERS OF 7
CHALLENGING CONVICTIONS

"Then said they, Come, and let us devise devices against Jeremiah; for the law shall not perish from the priest, nor counsel from the wise, nor the word from the prophet. Come, and let us smite him with the tongue, and let us not give heed to any of his words. "

"Jeremiah 18:18

Persuading Israel to listen to YeHoVaH did not go well for Jeremiah. Even though he, carefully, spoke the words YeHoVaH put in his mouth, and even though the witness of the Holy Spirit accompanied him, repentance never arose in the hearts of the people of God. Instead, they conspired and schemed against Jeremiah, even as our opening text states, "let us devise devices against Jeremiah."

In accordance with the statement of the people in verse 18, "for the law shall not perish from the priest, nor counsel from the wise, nor the word from the prophet", they thought they had all they needed to properly live their religious life.

Jeremiah's warning to the priests, wise men, and prophets, of whom Jeremiah declared in need of correction, did not help the people because they failed to recognize their own departure from the Word of God.

Jeremiah 2:26-27

> "26 As the thief is ashamed when he is found, so is the house of Israel ashamed; they, their kings, their princes, and their priests, and their prophets, 27 Saying to a stock, Thou [art] my father; and to a stone, Thou hast brought me forth: for they have turned [their] back unto me, and not [their] face: but in the time of their trouble they will say, Arise, and save us. "

Priests seeking counsel and giving praise to a stock or a stone, although offensive to God, seemed not a problem for the people. Obviously, their instructions in the practices of their faith seriously lacked proper insight. Instead of soul searching before YeHoVaH, they decided another course of action. "Come, and let us smite him with the tongue, and let us not give heed to any of his words." Jeremiah 18:18 Simply put, they decided to ruin his reputation, using slander to ignite trouble against Jeremiah. In that way, they stood united, paying no attention to Jeremiah's words.

As far as the people go, from what we read in Jeremiah, it appears that it did not enter their minds to sit down and reason with Jeremiah, to see where their leaders, priests and advisors just might be wrong! If they had done so, surely Jeremiah would gladly show them the places where their leaders failed to properly interpret what God desired. Jeremiah, due to his understanding of God and the prophetic call on his life, could have pointed out the places where they added their own interpretation, or places whereby their tradition, they nullified the word of God. As it stood at that time, every time the prophet, Jeremiah, spoke, challenges arose for all: prophet, leaders, and people!

Jeremiah, as the prophet, faced the challenges of an unrepented people. As the leaders and people encountered the Holy Spirit's fire, which empowered Jeremiah's preaching, they reacted with an adverse effect to God's convicting power of sin. Consequently, the people of Judah allowed their anger to rule their behaviour towards Jeremiah. Instead of repenting, they saw Jeremiah's words as the cause of their discomfort. First, their actions manifested in verbal assault and slander. Later, they displayed their anger with physical abuse towards Jeremiah, with situations designed to kill him.

Pashur, a son of one of the priests, decided to confront Jeremiah and solve the problem of this bothersome prophet. That confrontation brought Jeremiah great pain and humiliation:

Jeremiah 20:1-2
"1 Now Pashur the son of Immer the priest, who [was]
also chief governor in the house of YeHoVaH, heard that
Jeremiah prophesied these things. 2 Then Pashur smote
Jeremiah the prophet, and put him in the stocks that
[were] in the high gate of Benjamin, which [was] by the
house of YeHoVaH. "

To explain this treatment of Jeremiah in greater detail,
let us look at the word, "smote" in verse 2. That word
is נָכָה[44] (naw-kaw'). Elsewhere, KJV translators
interpret that word as stripes.

Deuteronomy 25:3
"3 Forty stripes he may give him, [and] not exceed: lest,
[if] he should exceed, and beat him above these with
many stripes, then thy brother should seem vile unto
thee. "

The similarity of the two words suggest that they beat
Jeremiah with 40 stripes of a whip, [45] and then, to add
more pain and humiliation, they put him in the stocks
on public display.

---

[44] Strong's Concordance, Hebrew word # 5221
[45] That was the suggested punishment with scourging, and while
we are not told this, due to the anger raging at Jeremiah, he most
likely received all the law allowed.

"Stocks" in Hebrew [46]מַהְפֶּכֶת, (mah-peh'-keth) means either prison, or some sort of containment where the body is twisted, which brings the victim great pain.

Pashur, this priest who Jeremiah called a false prophet, implemented this horrible ordeal upon Jeremiah and then, in the morning, went to release Jeremiah from the stocks. Perhaps, he felt Jeremiah, after enduring such pain and humiliation, would disappear into oblivion, never to prophesy again. However, upon releasing Jeremiah, he found his tortuous deeds did not deter Jeremiah. Instead of any expected remorse or retreat, Pashur met with a true word of a God-ordained prophet.

Jeremiah 20:3-6
   "3 And it came to pass on the morrow, that Pashur brought forth Jeremiah out of the stocks. Then said Jeremiah unto him, YeHoVaH hath not called thy name Pashur, but Magormissabib. 4 For thus saith YeHoVaH, Behold, I will make thee a terror to thyself, and to all thy friends: and they shall fall by the sword of their enemies, and thine eyes shall behold [it]: and I will give all Judah into the hand of the king of Babylon, and he shall carry them captive into Babylon, and shall slay them with the sword. 5 Moreover I will deliver all the strength of this city, and all the labours thereof,

---

[46] Strong's Concordance, Hebrew word # 4115

and all the precious things thereof, and all the treasures of the kings of Judah will I give into the hand of their enemies, which shall spoil them, and take them, and carry them to Babylon. 6 And thou, Pashur, and all that dwell in thine house shall go into captivity: and thou shalt come to Babylon, and there thou shalt die, and shalt be buried there, thou, and all thy friends, to whom thou hast prophesied lies. "

After pronouncing God's judgment upon Pashur, the false prophet, we hear of Jeremiah's agony as he speaks to YeHoVaH regarding his own thoughts:

Jeremiah 20: 7-8
"7 O YEHOVAH[47], thou hast deceived me, and I was deceived: thou art stronger than I, and hast prevailed: I am in derision daily, every one mocketh me. 8 For since I spake, I cried out, I cried violence and spoil; because the word of YeHoVaH was made a reproach unto me, and a derision, daily. "

Do these words, *"O YeHoVaH, thou hast deceived me,"* reflect a possible concept of God's promise which Jeremiah misunderstood? Did Jeremiah think God prohibited his deliverance into the hands of his

---

[47] Word is in all capitals, signifying its God's Covenant name. Same as when you see GOD, (all capitals). It is God's Covenant name.

oppressor? Did YeHoVaH, in Jeremiah's mind, promise Jeremiah a physically, pain free ministry?

On the surface, it might seem to be so! However, God's promise of enemies not prevailing manifested in Jeremiah's life amidst physical trauma and abuse. YeHoVaH gave Jeremiah strength to endure the horrible ordeals others forced upon him. Adversaries of Jeremiah tried to wound his body, his emotions, and the depth of his soul, however, Jeremiah arose from every encounter without bitterness, self-pity, rejection, or retaliation. God's strength kept Jeremiah alive in spirit, soul, and in body, able to stand and continue to proclaim God's Word in love, untainted by man's abuse.

How awesome is that in both YeHoVaH and His faithful prophet!

After Jeremiah's release from his ordeal with Pashur, Jeremiah reflects upon the problems of speaking God's Word:

Jeremiah 20: 9-13
"9 Then I said, I will not make mention of him, nor speak any more in his name. But [his word] was in mine heart as a burning fire shut up in my bones, and I was weary with forbearing, and I could not [stay].

10 For I heard the defaming of many, fear on every side. Report, [say they], and we will report it. All my familiars watched for my halting, [saying], Peradventure he will be enticed, and we shall prevail against him, and we shall take our revenge on him.

11 But YeHoVaH [is] with me as a mighty terrible one: therefore my persecutors shall stumble, and they shall not prevail: they shall be greatly ashamed; for they shall not prosper: [their] everlasting confusion shall never be forgotten. 12 But, O YEHOVAH of hosts, that triest the righteous, [and] seest the reins and the heart, let me see thy vengeance on them: for unto thee have I opened my cause. 13 Sing unto YeHoVaH, praise ye YeHoVaH: for he hath delivered the soul of the poor from the hand of evildoers. "

Jeremiah suffered more than words might describe as he proclaimed God's Word to Judah.   Some of Jeremiah's suffering included continuous slander against his word and character, physical beatings, imprisonment, even being abandoned to a place of death, from which he narrowly escaped[48]. We hear that his friends and family rejected him, too[49]. Yet, his faith clung to the One who alone offered him a true deliverance, and Jeremiah looked to the only One worthy to bring forth judgment and justice. He kept

---

[48] *Jeremiah 38:10*
[49] *Jeremiah 20:10*

his eyes on YeHoVaH and His ability to repay. In that way, Jeremiah guarded his heart against bitterness and vengeance. When he spoke God's Word, they were clean of personal agendas!

Today, many who experience persecution, *(or see another person persecuted)*, might wonder why this sort of thing happens. Some believers think that after they speak God's Word, God's favour means a total escape from the clutches of all problems or retaliation arising from the Word spoken. *Persecution does not mean God's disfavour.* Rather, if those words truly originated in the heart of the Father and came forth by God's order and fire of the Holy Spirit, it means the offending one's disfavour in God's eyes.

Such preachers of God's Word, who experience persecution for a true word of God, live within a category about which Yeshua spoke:

Luke 21:12-19
"12 But before all these, they shall lay their hands on you, and persecute [you], delivering [you] up to the synagogues, and into prisons, being brought before kings and rulers for my name's sake. 13 And it shall turn to you for a testimony. 14 Settle [it] therefore in your hearts, not to meditate before what ye shall answer: 15 For I will give you a mouth and wisdom, which all your adversaries shall not be able to gainsay

nor resist. 16 And ye shall be betrayed both by parents, and brethren, and kinsfolks, and friends; and [some] of you shall they cause to be put to death. 17 And ye shall be hated of all [men] for my name's sake. 18 But there shall not an hair of your head perish. 19 In your patience possess ye your souls. "

"In your patience possess your souls." In other words, keep your faith, hang in there and do not give up. Remember, that person is in good company with those saints of old! We must learn to think like Jeremiah when he uttered, "for he hath delivered the soul of the poor from the hand of the evil doers"[50].

Beloved reader, as we open our mouth to declare the Word of YeHoVaH, even in circumstances that seem favourable *(such as within our own familiar setting)* or unfavourable, *(such as a public forum)*, let us remember God's advice to Jeremiah: ***"Don't look at their faces".***[51] To look at faces tempts one to buy into the fear of man. Instead, seek God's favour and approval. In doing so, one walks away with a greater peace, and if persecution comes, vengeance and retaliation is, *easier,* left with God, for He is your measuring stick of success.

---

[50] *Jeremiah 20:13*
[51] A paraphrase of *Jeremiah 1:17*

In reflecting on the life of Jeremiah, remember that God called him to prophesy to a society with hardened hearts and broken commitments to God's covenant, surrounded by false teachers and prophets who reinforced the error. Let's remember that as Jeremiah experienced a challenge on every front, he had a saving grace to which we can adhere.

Jeremiah's saving grace was not the thought of escaping pain, affliction of unfair punishment, nor the removal of all opposition from his life. *Jeremiah's saving grace* rested in the pleasure of his God, YeHoVaH. His mind, heart, and soul, he fixed to speak YeHoVaH's Word alone, untainted by human retributions. Jeremiah disallowed bitterness to grow in his heart but allowed recompense and vengeance on his adversaries to come from the hand of the only One who weighs out the heart.

Jeremiah's ministry proved truthful, in the long run. His words, spoken from the heart of God, rang true. They stood the test of time. His fearless approach to preach and speak the Word of God, even facing the possibility of death, testifies to the strength YeHoVaH implemented within him. It gives a great example of how God can keep those who trust in Him.

In looking at Jeremiah's opponents, we might also remember they felt the challenge of the fire of the

Almighty. They experienced the conviction of sin yet refused to repent and receive God's forgiveness. This reaction often comes to those who oppose the truth. If you experience this, remember, the Word of God is conflicting to them. In your prayers for them, you might add a comment asking YeHoVaH to help them yield to the truth. Only God knows whether they will relent and serve Him!

MATTERS OF
DRASTIC DEALINGS

8

"8 Now it came to pass, when Jeremiah had made an end of speaking all that YeHoVaH had commanded [him] to speak unto all the people, that the priests and the prophets and all the people took him, saying, Thou shalt surely die. 9 Why hast thou prophesied in the name of YeHoVaH, saying, This house shall be like Shiloh, and this city shall be desolate without an inhabitant? And all the people were gathered against Jeremiah in the house of YeHoVaH."

Jeremiah 26:8-9

To prophesy in the name of YeHoVaH, a person took a risk. In accordance with Jewish Law, the Word of YeHoVaH prophesied possesses certain earmarks to receive approval. According to traditions, normally prophets spoke in the house of YeHoVaH. Their words, carefully recorded by scribes, must come to pass as predicted. While that seems obvious, due to the timeframe of prophetic words, some prophecies might not enjoy immediate fulfillment. Nevertheless, until the prophet's word showed verification, the leaders did not authenticate it as from YeHoVaH. From that, some might conclude, that was the main attribute of a prophetic word was its accuracy. While that aspect of the prophetic word stands the test of time, God gave another indicator, which few remember:

Deuteronomy 13:1-5
> *"1 If there arise among you a prophet, or a dreamer of dreams, and giveth thee a sign or a wonder, 2 And the sign or the wonder come to pass, whereof he spake unto thee, saying, Let us go after other gods, which thou hast not known, and let us serve them; 3 Thou shalt not hearken unto the words of that prophet, or that dreamer of dreams: for YeHoVaH your God proveth you, to know whether ye love YeHoVaH your God with all your heart and with all your soul.*

> *4 Ye shall walk after YeHoVaH your God, and fear him, and keep his commandments, and obey his voice, and ye shall serve him, and cleave unto him. 5 And that prophet, or that dreamer of dreams, shall be put to death; because he hath spoken to turn [you] away from YeHoVaH your God, which brought you out of the land of Egypt, and redeemed you out of the house of bondage, to thrust thee out of the way which YeHoVaH thy God commanded thee to walk in. So shalt thou put the evil away from the midst of thee. "*

In this passage we hear of signs that come to pass, however, the motive of this prophesier is identified as an invitation to follow other gods. Therefore, validation of the Word from YeHoVaH comes with more than a prophesy's fulfillment! The bottom-line points to whom the prophetic voice draws its listening audience. Remember this important aspect of the true Word of God, as well as its fulfillment:

Deuteronomy 13:2-4

"And the sign or the wonder come to pass, whereof he spake unto thee, saying, Let us go after other gods, which thou hast not known, and let us serve them; Thou shalt not hearken unto the words of that prophet, or that dreamer of dreams: for YeHoVaH your God proveth you, to know whether ye love YeHoVaH your God with all your heart and with all your soul. Ye shall walk after YeHoVaH your God, and fear him, and keep his commandments, and obey his voice, and ye shall serve him, and cleave unto him".

YeHoVaH tests His people, in this manner, to bring out in the open the loyalty of a person's heart. If their heart's focus is on Him alone, they will not leave their faith in Him. If, however, their heart waivers, they will choose to follow another, who seems to be powerful by the demonstration of the fulfilled word. When they leave the truth and go astray, God shows what treasures His people held as dear, including why they served Him[52].

This passage reminds us of another thing to remember. Words of the true prophets, in times past, often took time to fulfill. Many of Jeremiah's prophetic utterances fell into that category, such as the promised restoration of Israel found in the later chapters of the book.

Often, during Jeremiah's lifetime, his statements of judgment, such as the Babylonian captivity, seemed unfulfilled in the timeframe the people expected. Often onlookers and critics mistook YeHoVaH's mercy manifesting as delayed judgment as Jeremiah's mistake. However, Jeremiah's word did stand the test of time!

ROOT OF JEREMIAH'S ORACLES:

When Jerusalem underwent its first siege by Nebuchadnezzar, Daniel, when taken captive to Babylon, kept Jeremiah's words close to his heart. Daniel knew 70 years must pass before Jerusalem's rebuilding project occurred. This was Jeremiah's word

---

[52] In our world today, people do not often literally say, "go and serve other gods", nevertheless, they invite people to follow them. Then, they lead others away from the cross, away from the truth, and in the end, away from the Father, Who sent the Son. The true test of a prophet of God is that of his/her service to God alone, and the focus on others following that same service to God alone.

to Jerusalem, and in those early years before the siege, Daniel's ears heard it.

Daniel 9:2
"In the first year of his reign,[53] I Daniel understood by books the number of the years, whereof the word of YeHoVaH came to Jeremiah the prophet, that he would accomplish seventy years in the desolations of Jerusalem. "

Here, we see Daniel verifying Jeremiah as a prophet, and speaking out the prophecy, which Daniel trusted without a shadow of a doubt, and found too, that YeHoVaH verified as truth.

Even though, in Jeremiah's earlier years, some prophesies fulfillment came in a delayed frame of time, eventually, all he decreed about that time occurred. What Jeremiah decreed about the future when God calls His people back to God, we see fulfilled in our time! However, in all Jeremiah's prophesies, he called God's people to repent and return to the true God of Abraham, Isaac, and Jacob.[54]

---

[53] Reign of Darius, the son of Ahasuerus.

[54] Let the reader understand: Yeshua, as God's Prophet, came to bring YeHoVaH's people *back to the Father*. He said that He was the door that leads to eternal life. That life begins by accepting God's provided payment for sin, and then, recipients enter a life with the Father, through the Son. If Yeshua came to draw others

"*Jeremiah 3:12*

> *Go and proclaim these words toward the north, and say, Return, thou backsliding Israel, saith YeHoVaH; [and] I will not cause mine anger to fall upon you: for I [am] merciful, saith YeHoVaH, [and] I will not keep [anger] for ever.* "

Jeremiah 3:22

> *"Return, ye backsliding children, [and] I will heal your backslidings. Behold, we come unto thee; for thou [art] YeHoVaH our God.* "

Jeremiah 4:1

> *"If thou wilt return, O Israel, saith YeHoVaH, return unto me: and if thou wilt put away thine abominations out of my sight, then shalt thou not remove.* "

These three passages show the focus of Jeremiah, who pointed God's people to their rightful King, YeHoVaH.

Here is another:

---

away from the Father, by starting a new religion, as many believe He did, then God's Word classifies Him as a false prophet! Remember, Yeshua did not come to start a new religion. He came to bring all mankind to the Father, to the God of Abraham, Isaac, and Jacob.

Jeremiah 18:11-17

"11 Now therefore go to, speak to the men of Judah, and to the inhabitants of Jerusalem, saying, Thus saith YeHoVaH; Behold, I frame evil against you, and devise a device against you: return ye now every one from his evil way, and make your ways and your doings good. 12 And they said, There is no hope: but we will walk after our own devices, and we will every one do the imagination of his evil heart.

13 Therefore thus saith YeHoVaH; Ask ye now among the heathen, who hath heard such things: the virgin of Israel hath done a very horrible thing. 14 Will [a man] leave the snow of Lebanon [which cometh] from the rock of the field? [or] shall the cold flowing waters that come from another place be forsaken? 15 Because my people hath forgotten me, they have burned incense to vanity, and they have caused them to stumble in their ways [from] the ancient paths, to walk in paths, [in] a way not cast up; 16 To make their land desolate, [and] a perpetual hissing; every one that passeth thereby shall be astonished, and wag his head. 17 I will scatter them as with an east wind before the enemy; I will shew them the back, and not the face, in the day of their calamity. "

Jeremiah, commanded by YeHoVaH to speak to the men of Judah and all that inhabit that land of Israel, prophesied evil on the near horizon because they refused to turn to God. In fact, they brazenly declared they had no hope in YeHoVaH, therefore they went after what they desired and followed the imagination of their heart.

This trend to toss out YeHoVaH and embrace other gods appalled YeHoVaH. Even amongst the heathen nations, steeped in abominable practices, none in their heathen practices[55] advocated replacing the worship of their forefathers, yet the virgin daughter of Israel did so! Clean flowing waters rushing out from a rock is pure, refreshing, and delightful, as is a similar water that flows from a cold stream. Only a fool forsakes such a source of water and turns to a dirty stream to sustain them! Yet Israel did that exact thing!

Israel forsook the Living God[56], Whose waters gave pure, holy, refreshing, and life-giving drink. They burned incense to vanity, which caused them to stumble in their ways to walk in unknown paths. Like a person wandering in the dark, they stumbled along

---

[55] The key word here is "heathen". Heathens exchanging their faith for YeHoVaH is not the consideration here. It is heathens practicing their faith, not knowing about YeHoVaH. They, on their own, would not think of forsaking the worship of their forefathers.

[56] *"Hearken to me, ye that follow after righteousness, ye that seek YeHoVaH: look unto the rock [whence] ye are hewn, and to the hole of the pit [whence] ye are digged."* (Isaiah 51:1).

their way, moving further and further into darkness. Indeed, their darkness led them to stray far away from the ancient paths given by the true prophets of God. Therein was life, however, they treated that life recklessly, even as worthless. Instead, they chose death. Thus, God slated their land for a time of desolation, and in that state a continual mocking. Amazement of its end catches everyone who passes by. Their heads shake in disbelief.

God promises, through Jeremiah, to scatter Israel with an east wind[57] before their very enemy. He shows them His back and not His face in the day of their calamity! Such is the price for their idolatry. Such is the price for walking away from the living waters of YeHoVaH. Such is the price for disrespecting the best and accepting something of far lesser value in its place! Such is the price for embracing the earth, its values, its treasures to forsake the higher call to serve the Living God in righteousness and truth.

Jeremiah's message declared drastic dealings with a rebellious people. This fact, partially, explains the delay in judgments coming forth. YeHoVaH, in His

---

[57] Note, an east wind rescued them from slavery, but now it scatters them! *Exodus 14:21 " And Moses stretched out his hand over the sea; and YeHoVaH caused the sea to go back by a strong **east wind** all that night, and made the sea dry land, and the waters were divided. "*

mercy, also delays the coming doom, to give people opportunity to repent:

2 Peter 3:9
> "9 *The Lord is not slack concerning his promise, as some men count slackness; but is longsuffering to us-ward, not willing that any should perish, but that all should come to repentance.* "

Let us remember, today, when weighing prophetic words through the filter of discernment, give room for God's mercy! Surely, if *our life* laid in the balance, we would appreciate the additional time to get right with God![58]

---

[58] Today, let's remember to look at such prophetic words of modern prophets with the discernment of the Spirit of God and the heart of the Father as prophetically declared judgments might be delayed.

MATTERS OF
OVERCOMING OBSTACLES

9

---

*"He that overcometh shall inherit all things; and I will be his
God, and he shall be my son."*

Revelation 21:7

Jeremiah, God's prophet and servant in Jerusalem,
endured conflict amongst a contrary people, even
unto the day of his death, which was by stoning in
the land of Egypt. Into this foreign land, Jeremiah
came, but not by the orders of YeHoVaH! It happened
this way:

Jeremiah 43:1-7
*"1 And it came to pass, that when Jeremiah had made an
end of speaking unto all the people all the words of
YeHoVaH their God, for which YeHoVaH their God had
sent him to them, even all these words, 2 Then spake
Azariah the son of Hoshaiah, and Johanan the son of
Kareah, and all the proud men, saying unto Jeremiah,
Thou speakest falsely: YeHoVaH our God hath not sent
thee to say, Go not into Egypt to sojourn there:*

*3 But Baruch the son of Neriah setteth thee on against us,
for to deliver us into the hand of the Chaldeans, that they
might put us to death, and carry us away captives into
Babylon. 4 So Johanan the son of Kareah, and all the*

*captains of the forces, and all the people, obeyed not the voice of YeHoVaH, to dwell in the land of Judah. 5 But Johanan the son of Kareah, and all the captains of the forces, took all the remnant of Judah, that were returned from all nations, whither they had been driven, to dwell in the land of Judah; 6 Even men, and women, and children, and the king's daughters, and every person that Nebuzaradan the captain of the guard had left with Gedaliah the son of Ahikam the son of Shaphan, **and Jeremiah the prophet**, and Baruch the son of Neriah. 7 So they came into the land of Egypt: for they obeyed not the voice of YeHoVaH: thus came they even to Tahpanhes. "*

Jeremiah, forcibly taken to Egypt, continued to prophecy in that land, even words against their present-day government.   Jeremiah promised the destruction of Pharaoh's house, property, destruction of false gods of Egypt, and more![59] In payment for his prophetic words in Egypt, according to tradition, Jeremiah was stoned to death.

A review of Jeremiah's life shows continual controversy from the time YeHoVaH called him to preach.   Jeremiah's success in serving YeHoVaH, through all that he suffers, lies in the words of the promise of YeHoVaH to Jeremiah:

---

[59] *Jeremiah 43:8-13*

Jeremiah 1:18-19
> *"18 For, behold, I have made thee this day a defenced city, and an iron pillar, and brasen walls against the whole land, against the kings of Judah, against the princes thereof, against the priests thereof, and against the people of the land. 19 And they shall fight against thee; but they shall not prevail against thee; for I am with thee, saith YeHoVaH, to deliver thee. "*

Jeremiah 6:27
> *"I have set thee for a tower and a fortress among my people, that thou mayest know and try their way. "*

Jeremiah 15:20
> *"And I will make thee unto this people a fenced brasen wall: and they shall fight against thee, but they shall not prevail against thee: for I am with thee to save thee and to deliver thee, saith YeHoVaH. "*

At first, it seems YeHoVaH's promise meant Jeremiah's physical safety, however, after reviewing Jeremiah's life, we see its meaning went deeper. Jeremiah never caved, never lost his faith and trust in YeHoVaH as he endured the tortuous ordeals thrust upon him by the people of Judah, the priests, the kings, or any who inflicted him. Jeremiah stood faithful to YeHoVaH!

Indeed, Jeremiah, the weeping prophet as he is called, falls nicely into the category of the brave in the Christian Hall of Fame:

Hebrews 11:32-40

"32 And what shall I more say? for the time would fail me to tell of Gedeon, and [of] Barak, and [of] Samson, and [of] Jephthae; [of] David also, and Samuel, and [of] the prophets: 33 Who through faith subdued kingdoms, wrought righteousness, obtained promises, stopped the mouths of lions, 34 Quenched the violence of fire, escaped the edge of the sword, out of weakness were made strong, waxed valiant in fight, turned to flight the armies of the aliens. 35 Women received their dead raised to life again: and others were tortured, not accepting deliverance; that they might obtain a better resurrection:

36 And others had trial of [cruel] mockings and scourgings, yea, moreover of bonds and imprisonment: 37 They were stoned,[60] they were sawn asunder, were tempted, were slain with the sword: they wandered about in sheepskins and goatskins; being destitute, afflicted, tormented; 38 (Of whom the world was not worthy:) they wandered in deserts, and [in] mountains, and [in] dens and caves of the earth. 39 And these all, having obtained a good report through faith, received not the promise: 40 God having provided

---

[60] Some believe this is clear reference to the death of Jeremiah.

some better thing for us, that they without us should not be made perfect. "

For those with eyes to see, Jeremiah stood for righteousness in his day amidst the people of Judah. His faith in his God, his ability to trust and keep on trusting, to prophecy no matter the consequences, shows evidence that he was that brazen wall YeHoVaH promised. Jeremiah was that tower and fortress amongst God's people!

AN EXAMPLE FOR OTHERS:

Jeremiah's life, forged by God, stood as a testimony to all who looked upon him. Those of his day missed their opportunity to embrace a chosen beacon of light for their time, yet we today, can embrace the full meaning of this amazing servant of YeHoVaH! We, the believers of today, whether living in peaceful or tumultuous times, can look at the tower of strength and brazen wall fastened by YeHoVaH, as an example to stand for righteousness in our day.

As we do, we keep in mind that Jeremiah's destiny, His anointed prophetic call from YeHoVaH, commenced before his breath on this earth began! YeHoVaH made that clear in His first encounter with Jeremiah:

Jeremiah 1:4-5
> *"4 Then the word of YeHoVaH came unto me, saying, 5*
> *Before I formed thee in the belly I knew thee; and before*
> *thou camest forth out of the womb I sanctified thee, [and]*
> *I ordained thee a prophet unto the nations. "*

What YeHoVaH did for Jeremiah to help him complete his destiny, He does for all:

Acts 10:34
> *"34 Then Peter opened [his] mouth, and said, Of a*
> *truth I perceive that God is no respecter of persons: "*

YeHoVaH, dear one, knows your destiny. He fashioned you in your mother's womb to attain it! He knew, well ahead of time, the generation in which you would live out your years. He knew the righteousness or unrighteousness of that generation. He knew the tears you would shed, and the pain you would endure for His name's sake! He knew the testing, the trials, the mocking, the cruel slander, and everything you would suffer!

Like Jeremiah, he formed you to handle it all
With His strength to help you endure!

Paul, the Apostle, put it this way:

124

2 Corinthians 12:7-10

> *"7 And lest I should be exalted above measure through the abundance of the revelations, there was given to me a thorn in the flesh, the messenger of Satan to buffet me, lest I should be exalted above measure. 8 For this thing I besought the Lord thrice, that it might depart from me.*
>
> *9 And he said unto me, My grace is sufficient for thee: for my strength is made perfect in weakness. Most gladly therefore will I rather glory in my infirmities, that the power of Christ may rest upon me. 10 Therefore I take pleasure in infirmities, in reproaches, in necessities, in persecutions, in distresses for Christ's sake: for when I am weak, then am I strong. "*

A great focus from this scripture, in recap says, *"9 My grace is sufficient for thee: for my strength is made perfect in weakness. Most gladly therefore will I rather glory in my infirmities, that the power of Christ may rest upon me. 10 Therefore I take pleasure in infirmities, in reproaches, in necessities, in persecutions, in distresses for Christ's sake: for when I am weak, then am I strong."*

Perhaps, Paul took his lessons from Jeremiah! Of this we do not know, but we do know that YeHoVaH has not changed! As He helped Jeremiah, even made him a tower for his own generation, so too can He help you!

Dear one, as we close out this section on Jeremiah's ministry, looking at his character, his call, his strengths, and weaknesses, it is time to apply the lessons learned to our life! Let us take some time and give every opposition, every contention, every persecution you've endured over to the Master for His Touch! [61]

Of a certainty, it is time to praise Him for how He's kept you, made you strong, planted your feet on solid ground! It is time to thank Him for forging strength in you to overcome all obstacles until the day you see Him face to face! It is time to rejoice that, like Jeremiah, you are a brazen wall, one who won't collapse in the day of adversity because your trust is in your God!

Beloved, let us look past the present moment into the face of our future when we stand before the One who redeemed us, strengthened us, and helped us to stand! Such focus will keep us above the circumstances and build in us the character, like Jeremiah, to endure until the end.

Revelation 21:7

"He that overcometh shall inherit all things; and I will be his God, and he shall be my son."

---

[61] Release all people involved, as well, if you have not done so!

***

In the next section we will investigate God's answer to injustice. We will see how His forgiveness, while readily extended to Israel, met with disregard. As this study ends, we will see YeHoVaH's amazing forgiveness and promised restoration of Israel.

Together, we will focus our eyes on the God we serve, Who reigns beyond the circumstances and Whose greatness soars beyond our wildest dreams!

***

The Jeremiah Generation

SECTION 3:

INJUSTICE ROMOVED

(Punishment & Promised Restoration)

MATTERS OF
REQUIRED RECOMPENSE

10

Part 1

"29 O that they were wise, [that] they understood this, [that] they would consider their latter end! 30 How should one chase a thousand, and two put ten thousand to flight, except their Rock had sold them, and YeHoVaH had shut them up? 31 For their rock [is] not as our Rock, even our enemies themselves [being] judges. 32 For their vine [is] of the vine of Sodom, and of the fields of Gomorrah: their grapes [are] grapes of gall, their clusters [are] bitter: 33 Their wine [is] the poison of dragons, and the cruel venom of asps. 34 [Is] not this laid up in store with me, [and] sealed up among my treasures? 35 To me [belongeth] vengeance, and recompence; their foot shall slide in [due] time: for the day of their calamity [is] at hand, and the things that shall come upon them make haste. "

Deuteronomy 32:29-35

YeHoVaH advises His people to look beyond the moment. He calls them to raise their eyes past their personal feelings, whether anger, anguish, or any erratic emotions. Let none of these be the inspiration to forward choices and responses. Rather, respond righteously. Remember their latter end! To do this is wisdom.

Throughout the book of Jeremiah, we see places where people responded to Jeremiah in the moment, allowing the circumstances to determine their response. Most did not seek YeHoVaH to determine if, indeed, He sent Jeremiah. Instead, they responded with indignation, offense and often fury as Jeremiah's words of correction came like fire into their ears:

Jeremiah 23:29

"Is not my word like as a fire? saith YeHoVaH; and like a **hammer** that breaketh the rock in pieces? "

A righteous response requires a time for all to come before YeHoVaH, in a serious searching of the soul to determine, if indeed, our actions offended Him[62]. Instead of this response, most in Jeremiah's time hurled accusations at him, threatened him and did him harm. For these things, YeHoVaH repaid. The intent of such actions on YeHoVaH's side came to the people as a recompense for their earlier actions.

REQUIRED RECOMPENSE:

Jeremiah records many aspects of God's promised recompense, or pay back, for certain individuals,

---

[62] Daily accounts with God are a great idea and produce much fruit in our relationship with the Almighty.

places, and circumstances. Let us look at some of these together: [63]

PASHUR:

Earlier, we read how Pashur, the son of Immer the priest, who also stood in the position of chief governor of YeHoVaH's house, heard Jeremiah's prophesies. In response, he smote Jeremiah and put him in the stocks in the high gate of Benjamin, which was by the house of YeHoVaH. Scripture goes on to say:

Jeremiah 20:3-6
  "3 And it came to pass on the morrow, that Pashur brought forth Jeremiah out of the stocks. Then said Jeremiah unto him, YeHoVaH hath not called thy name Pashur, but Magormissabib.   4 For thus saith YeHoVaH, Behold, I will make thee a terror to thyself, and to all thy friends: and they shall fall by the sword of their enemies, and thine eyes shall behold [it]: and I will give all Judah into the hand of the king of Babylon, and he shall carry them captive into Babylon, and shall slay them with the sword.

---

[63] There are many places in the book of Jeremiah where God promises recompense. We cannot have time to do everything, so these are but highlights. If you wish to learn more, look through the accompanying workbook to locate the chapters ready for your analysis. Perhaps, you can recap the promised recompenses as a theme as you read through the book.

> *5 Moreover I will deliver all the strength of this city,*
> *and all the labours thereof, and all the precious things*
> *thereof, and all the treasures of the kings of Judah will I*
> *give into the hand of their enemies, which shall spoil*
> *them, and take them, and carry them to Babylon. 6 And*
> *thou, Pashur, and all that dwell in thine house shall go*
> *into captivity: and thou shalt come to Babylon, and*
> *there thou shalt die, and shalt be buried there, thou, and*
> *all thy friends, to whom thou hast prophesied lies. "*

Here, we have a pronouncement of YeHoVaH about
Pashur:

- *A Name change*: Pashur, as his father named him,
  means freedom. As a name describes the person,
  YeHoVaH gave Pashur a new name to describe
  him, Magormissabib, meaning terror on every side.
  His life of freedom stops and a life of terror on
  every side replaces it.
- *A Life change*: Pashur a terror to himself, becomes a
  terror to all his friends. They will fall by the sword
  of their enemies, and Pashur shall see it happen.
- *A National change:* YeHoVaH gives all Judah into
  the hands of the king of Babylon, who invades it,
  plunders it, and carries everything away to
  Babylon, slaying many by the sword.
- *A City change:* The city of Jerusalem, along with its
  great strength and economic structure, fails. All the

precious things and treasures of the King of Judah, YeHoVaH gives as spoil to Babylon to carry away.

• *A Family change:* Pashur, and all in his house no longer enjoy freedom, for God sends them into captivity in Babylon, where he, family, and friends, will die and be buried.

Pashur rejected the words of YeHoVaH, through Jeremiah the prophet. He also prophesied "freedom" to the people in Judah, causing them not to repent, nor trust in the words of the true prophet of God. He caused his listeners to trust in a lie. For these things and more, as well as Pashur's own refusal to repent, God repaid Pashur.

HANANIAH

In Jeremiah Chapter 27, YeHoVaH instructs his prophet to send yokes to certain kings, including the King of Judah. Along with the yoke, this message comes to every king:

Jeremiah 27: 4b)-11
"4 b) Thus saith YeHoVaH of hosts, the God of Israel; Thus shall ye say unto your masters; 5 I have made the earth, the man and the beast that [are] upon the ground, by my great power and by my outstretched arm, and have given it unto whom it seemed meet unto me. 6 And now have I given all these lands into the hand of Nebuchadnezzar the king of Babylon, my

*servant; and the beasts of the field have I given him
also to serve him. 7 And all nations shall serve him,
and his son, and his son's son, until the very time of
his land come: and then many nations and great kings
shall serve themselves of him.*

*8 And it shall come to pass, [that] the nation and
kingdom which will not serve the same
Nebuchadnezzar the king of Babylon, and that will
not put their neck under the yoke of the king of
Babylon, that nation will I punish, saith YeHoVaH,
with the sword, and with the famine, and with the
pestilence, until I have consumed them by his hand.
9 Therefore hearken not ye to your prophets, nor to
your diviners, nor to your dreamers, nor to your
enchanters, nor to your sorcerers, which speak unto
you, saying, Ye shall not serve the king of Babylon:
10 For they prophesy a lie unto you, to remove you
far from your land; and that I should drive you out,
and ye should perish. 11 But the nations that bring
their neck under the yoke of the king of Babylon, and
serve him, those will I let remain still in their own
land, saith YeHoVaH; and they shall till it, and dwell
therein. "*

In addition to these words to the King of Judah,
Zedekiah, Jeremiah adds the destruction coming to
Jerusalem. That destruction included the ransacking

of the temple and its precious articles.[64] In addition, Jeremiah warns Zedekiah not to listen to the prophets which tell him Jerusalem and all within overcome Nebuchadnezzar's attack on the city.

Jeremiah 27: 12-18

"*12 I spake also to Zedekiah king of Judah according to all these words, saying, Bring your necks under the yoke of the king of Babylon, and serve him and his people, and live. 13 Why will ye die, thou and thy people, by the sword, by the famine, and by the pestilence, as YeHoVaH hath spoken against the nation that will not serve the king of Babylon? 14 Therefore hearken not unto the words of the prophets that speak unto you, saying, Ye shall not serve the king of Babylon: for they prophesy a lie unto you. 15 For I have not sent them, saith YeHoVaH, yet they prophesy a lie in my name; that I might drive you out, and that ye might perish, ye, and the prophets that prophesy unto you.   16 Also I spake to the priests and to all this people, saying, Thus saith YeHoVaH; Hearken not to the words of your prophets that prophesy unto you, saying, Behold, the vessels of YeHoVaH's house shall now shortly be brought again from Babylon: for they prophesy a lie unto you. 17 Hearken not unto them; serve the king of Babylon, and live: wherefore should this city be laid waste? 18 But if they [be] prophets, and if the word of YeHoVaH be with them, let them now*

---

[64] *Jeremiah 27:12-22*

make intercession to YeHoVaH of hosts, that the vessels
which are left in the house of YeHoVaH, and [in] the
house of the king of Judah, and at Jerusalem, go not to
Babylon. "

This clear word confronts the false prophets and others speaking lies to the king. Obviously, Jeremiah's words, which contradicts those of the courts of the king and his rulers, causes trouble. One of those false prophets, Hananiah, a trusted advisor and noted prophet of the court of the king retorts:

Jeremiah 28:2-4
"2 Thus speaketh YeHoVaH of hosts, the God of Israel,
saying, I have broken the yoke of the king of Babylon.
3 Within two full years will I bring again into this
place all the vessels of YeHoVaH's house, that
Nebuchadnezzar king of Babylon took away from this
place, and carried them to Babylon: 4 And I will bring
again to this place Jeconiah the son of Jehoiakim king
of Judah, with all the captives of Judah, that went into
Babylon, saith YeHoVaH: for I will break the yoke of
the king of Babylon. "

Then, as Hananiah continues, he breaks the yoke from the neck of Jeremiah, who wore it to demonstrate a point to the people, the king, rulers, and priests of their coming captivity. Then, Hananiah prophesies:

Jeremiah 28:11

> *"11 And Hananiah spake in the presence of all the people,
> saying, Thus saith YeHoVaH; Even so will I break the
> yoke of Nebuchadnezzar king of Babylon from the neck of
> all nations within the space of two full years. And the
> prophet Jeremiah went his way. "*

Then, the word of YeHoVaH comes to Jeremiah, after
Hananiah broke the yoke from the neck of Jeremiah:

Jeremiah 28:12-17

> *"12 Then the word of YeHoVaH came unto Jeremiah
> [the prophet], after that Hananiah the prophet had
> broken the yoke from off the neck of the prophet
> Jeremiah, saying, 13 Go and tell Hananiah, saying,
> Thus saith YeHoVaH; Thou hast broken the yokes of
> wood; but thou shalt make for them yokes of iron. 14
> For thus saith YeHoVaH of hosts, the God of Israel; I
> have put a yoke of iron upon the neck of all these
> nations, that they may serve Nebuchadnezzar king of
> Babylon; and they shall serve him: and I have given him
> the beasts of the field also.*
>
> *15 Then said the prophet Jeremiah unto Hananiah the
> prophet, Hear now, Hananiah; YeHoVaH hath not sent
> thee; but thou makest this people to trust in a lie. 16
> Therefore thus saith YeHoVaH; Behold, I will cast thee
> from off the face of the earth: this year thou shalt die,
> because thou hast taught rebellion against YeHoVaH.*

17 So Hananiah the prophet died the same year in the seventh month. "

Hananiah, a trusted prophet of the king, spoke falsely in the name of YeHoVaH. As he did, he made the situation much worse. Jeremiah, through his strong prophetic word, made it clear that YeHoVaH did not send Hananiah who caused the people to trust in a lie. Consequently, God would deal with Hananiah:

- Hananiah's life would end as God cast him off the face of the earth.
- Hananiah, died within the same year because he taught rebellion against YeHoVaH.

God takes these things seriously! Hananiah, a false prophet directly opposing the word of YeHoVaH, caused people to trust in a lie, and thus, he received a recompense for his actions from YeHoVaH, *and quickly!* Perhaps, this swift response gave the king and onlookers enough evidence of the truth of Jeremiah's word to believe his words, turn around, repent and live!

It is imperative that before a person speaks for God, they ensure God is really in it! It is not a light thing to prophesy in the name of YeHoVaH! Better to ensure one has stood in the counsel of the Almighty and know His heart and mind before opening the mouth and speaking on His behalf!

Jeremiah 23:17-22

"17 They say still unto them that despise me, YeHoVaH hath said, Ye shall have peace; and they say unto every one that walketh after the imagination of his own heart, No evil shall come upon you. 18 For who hath stood in the counsel of YeHoVaH, and hath perceived and heard his word? who hath marked his word, and heard [it]?

19 Behold, a whirlwind of YeHoVaH is gone forth in fury, even a grievous whirlwind: it shall fall grievously upon the head of the wicked. 20 The anger of YeHoVaH shall not return, until he have executed, and till he have performed the thoughts of his heart: in the latter days ye shall consider it perfectly.

21 I have not sent these prophets, yet they ran: I have not spoken to them, yet they prophesied. 22 But if they had stood in my counsel, and had caused my people to hear my words, then they should have turned them from their evil way, and from the evil of their doings. "

MATTERS OF
REQUIRED RECOMPENSE

11

Part 2

"16 Thus saith the LORD of hosts, Hearken not unto the words of the prophets that prophesy unto you: they make you vain: they speak a vision of their own heart, and not out of the mouth of the LORD. 17 They say still unto them that despise me, The LORD hath said, Ye shall have peace; and they say unto every one that walketh after the imagination of his own heart, No evil shall come upon you. 18 For who hath stood in the counsel of the LORD, and hath perceived and heard his word? who hath marked his word, and heard it? 19 Behold, a whirlwind of the LORD is gone forth in fury, even a grievous whirlwind: it shall fall grievously upon the head of the wicked. 20 The anger of the LORD shall not return, until he have executed, and till he have performed the thoughts of his heart: in the latter days ye shall consider it perfectly."

Jeremiah 23:16-20

Looking at the time of recompense, it is noteworthy to recognize that God, Himself, repays. Now, He may use a person, a nation, a calamity of earth, such as a flood, however, if one looks behind the scenes where God's recompense took place,

they will find YeHoVaH[65]! Such was the case with
Hananiah, and Pashur. Such was the case with the
ones reviewed in this chapter, namely, Shallum and
Zedekiah.

SHALLUM:

Shallum, the son of King Josiah, took the throne after
his father's death. Instead of sowing righteousness
into Israel, he sowed unrighteousness, incurring
YeHoVaH's hand of recompense.

Jeremiah 22:11-17

*"11 For thus saith YeHoVaH touching Shallum the son
of Josiah king of Judah, which reigned instead of Josiah
his father, which went forth out of this place; He shall
not return thither any more: 12 But he shall die in the
place whither they have led him captive, and shall see
this land no more. 13 Woe unto him that buildeth his
house by unrighteousness, and his chambers by wrong;
[that] useth his neighbour's service without wages, and
giveth him not for his work; 14 That saith, I will build
me a wide house and large chambers, and cutteth him
out windows; and [it is] cieled with cedar, and painted
with vermilion. 15 Shalt thou reign, because thou*

---

[65] This does not mean, by any stretch of the imagination, that
God's fury lays behind every flood or hurricane or calamity on
the earth! This comment simply means, there are times when
YeHoVaH uses these things, and in their function, the recompense
He promised arrives.

closest [thyself] in cedar? did not thy father eat and drink, and do judgment and justice, [and] then [it was] well with him? 16 He judged the cause of the poor and needy; then [it was] well [with him: was] not this to know me? saith YeHoVaH. 17 But thine eyes and thine heart [are] not but for thy covetousness, and for to shed innocent blood, and for oppression, and for violence, to do [it]. "

It is obvious from this passage that Shallum chose to execute his kingly duties in a manner most displeasing to the Almighty.

Shallum's idea of a king began with a love for an ostentatious lifestyle. He said in his heart that he would live in splendour, and so, he built himself a grand house. It had many rooms, with windows and cedar trims and wainscotings decorated with vermillion (red).

This expensive kingly dwelling, he built unrighteously. He ordered expensive supplies and employed skilled tradesmen to do the work for him, however, he refused to compensate the people for the supplies, and did not pay the workmen their wages. He took their labour for free as well as their goods. What means of income God gave to these workmen to provide for their families, Shallum robbed, when he refused to pay them[66].

YeHoVaH asks Shallum about the greatness of rule, questioning if it rested in his kingly surroundings? YeHoVaH admonished Shallum to consider his forefathers, which God considered righteous. Although, in Shallum's eyes, they did not dwell in great splendour, nevertheless, they righteously meted out judgment and justice. Therefore, they ate and drank well as God kept them in their kingly place.

On the other hand, Shallum held an incorrect focus, for he became caught up in external prosperity. He thought the king's surroundings made the greatness of the king. YeHoVaH tells him, through Jeremiah, what counts is the behaviour and righteous rule of a king's administration! No covetous heart, no shedding of innocent blood, nor the generating of oppression or violence impresses YeHoVaH! Rather, correctly judge the cause of the poor and needy, and administer true justice for that makes a great king.

---

[66] God despises these types of business deals, but the offence increases when people cheat others as they work on projects for God's own house! People of God, let us be careful when doing things at all times that we sow in righteousness, and especially careful as we do things unto God in His house and in His name.

Therefore, due to Shallum's sins against YeHoVaH and the people, his most precious building, that which he thought made him great, he would see no more. Rather, Shallum, under God's judgment, headed straight towards Babylon, with his hands and feet chained like a slave. As Shallum headed for captivity, the visual accomplishments of his reign, namely his beautiful palace built by the blood, sweat and tears of others, faded away in the distance behind him.

Shallum's legacy in the permanency of scripture records his unrighteous reign, which included oppression of the poor and needy, propagation of violence, and injustice. These activities of which he refused to repent, bought him a one-way ticket to a dark place in Babylonian captivity. As promised by YeHoVaH, through the words of Jeremiah, Shallum died in that prison[67] for kings in Babylon, without the mourning, weeping or burial due to a king.

Regarding that glamourous living quarters Shallum built himself, flames engulfed it as, many years later, Nebuchadnezzar's men burnt Jerusalem to the ground.

---

[67] Babylon, like many other conquering nations, respected the kings of other nations. Although they conquered them, if that king refused to pay tribute and serve under their rule, they were taken to prison. Usually, that prison, although dark, cold, and dreary, was not the same as the prison for criminals of lesser social status.

Shallum's goal for a powerful reign, which focused on elevating his own greatness, ended as a pile of ashes, which the wind blew into oblivion.

Shallum's life, and his sad ending in captivity in Babylon, stand as a witness to the outcome of unrighteous governments of any kind, whether it is a father over a household, an owner over a business, a pastor over a church, a mayor over a city, a premier over a province, or a prime minister over a nation. It is imperative that anyone in any form of leadership recognize their accountability to God for their actions. In fact, that is exactly why universities originally came into being. Knowing God's required behaviour, with its rewards for righteous and unrighteous behaviour, made room for accountability as they arose as rulers in their generation. These learning institutions focused, therefore, on a greater understanding of the Bible to prepare future lawmakers of nations to grasp God's intentions for them.

Unfortunately, over time, the focus of that superior educational system left its original moorings. Looking at the roots of higher education and moving forward, we see a progressive and gradual bending away from the Bible's code of ethics and its principles for justice and righteousness. Acknowledging such behaviour and continuing to move towards our society, today, we arrive at multi-level educational systems, governments, and even churches, which embrace humanistic and materialistic viewpoints above the written Word of the One Who gave nations life, in the first place.

Nevertheless, the Creator of all things still calls every person and nation to shift their eyes away from goals contrary to scripture. His Spirit calls all those with ears to hear to refocus wherever necessary and align with God's idea of justice and truth. Wisdom dictates for the nations of the world, *in every generation*, along with their rulers and people, **to remember Shallum, his goals, purpose, and end.** Weighing his life's focus and its reward by God's hand of judgment, warns us to seek the true value of this life. Contemplating Shallum's wicked actions and his end stand as a good lesson for all, especially for those who govern in any capacity. Such thoughts have the potential to produce good fruit, *if we apply the lesson shown here!*

ZEDEKIAH:

This man, Zedekiah, was the third son of Josiah and named Mattaniah. After Nebuchadnezzar broke down the walls of Jerusalem, he made that city subservient to Babylon and consequently, the nation, also. He crowned Mattaniah king, thus omitting the hand of the true prophet from God pouring a vial of anointing oil upon the chosen descendant of David. In addition, rather than a king using his own name, or one of his choice, showing his reign over a nation, Mattaniah[68] received a new name from Nebuchadnezzar, namely Zedekiah[69]. For a time, Zedekiah[70] paid tribute to Babylon, as the terms of his kingship required, but later he rebelled against the king of Babylon and the commitment to serve him. Zedekiah, through the false prophets, believed YeHoVaH to see Nebuchadnezzar's hand removed and Israel to rule as before the conquest of Jerusalem.

2 Chronicles 36:11-13
"11 Zedekiah [was] one and twenty years old when he began to reign, and reigned eleven years in Jerusalem. 12 And he did [that which was] evil in the sight of YeHoVaH his God, [and] humbled not himself before Jeremiah the prophet [speaking] from the mouth of YeHoVaH. 13 And he also rebelled against king Nebuchadnezzar, who had made him swear by God: but he stiffened his neck, and hardened his heart from turning unto YeHoVaH God of Israel. "

Zedekiah, as shown in the above scripture, did evil in the sight of YeHoVaH. Also, during his reign, the chief priests as well as the people sinned greatly. They embraced idols and their abominable practices, such as human sacrifices rooted in that idolatry. Also, they

---

[68] Mattaniah means gift of YeHoVaH.
[69] *2 Kings 24:17*
[70] Zedekiah means righteousness of YeHoVaH.

polluted the house of YeHoVaH by bringing idols into the temple in places dedicated solely to YeHoVaH. Some earlier prophets spoke out against these practices, as God 's compassion desired them to repent of their wickedness and seek YeHoVaH for forgiveness. Instead, they mocked these messengers of the Almighty, despised their words and abused the very prophets which God called to reach out to them. This they did until "there was no remedy".[71]

2 Chronicles 36:17-21

"17 Therefore he brought upon them the king of the Chaldees, who slew their young men with the sword in the house of their sanctuary, and had no compassion upon young man or maiden, old man, or him that stooped for age: he gave them all into his hand. 18 And all the vessels of the house of God, great and small, and the treasures of the house of YeHoVaH, and the treasures of the king, and of his princes; all these he brought to Babylon. 19 And they burnt the house of God, and brake down the wall of Jerusalem, and burnt all the palaces thereof with fire, and destroyed all the goodly vessels thereof. 20 And them that had escaped from the sword carried he away to Babylon; where they were servants to him and his sons until the reign of the kingdom of Persia: 21 To fulfil the word of YeHoVaH by the mouth of Jeremiah, until the land had enjoyed

---

[71] *2 Chronicles 36:16*

151

her sabbaths: for as long as she lay desolate she kept
sabbath, to fulfil threescore and ten years. "

As Jerusalem fell to Babylon, men, woman, and
children of all ages died by the sword of the enemy.
Those who did not die by the sword, Babylonian
soldiers took to Babylon. There the people remained
until God's seventy years passed[72], at which time a
remnant returned. In addition, Babylonian soldiers
ransacked God's house, removing the sacred vessels[73]
of God's house, taking them to Babylon. Then, they set
fire to the House of YeHoVaH, burning it to the
ground.

Babylon, so efficient in their conquering of the capital
city of Israel, Jerusalem, did not forget about its king,
who so strongly rebelled against Babylon. Zedekiah,
along with his sons, who tried desperately to escape,
nevertheless fell into the hands of Babylonian soldiers.
Zedekiah watched as Nebuchadnezzar's men slayed
the heirs to Zedekiah's throne with the sword. After
that, they blinded Zedekiah[74]. In accordance with
YeHoVaH's words, Zedekiah did not die with the
invasion of Jerusalem. Babylonian soldiers carried him
off to captivity where he died, just as Jeremiah foretold.

---

[72] This was an actual 70-year period of time.
[73] Not including the ark, and other objects in the Holy Place as
Jeremiah saw to their removal, hiding them in a cave
underground.
[74] *Jeremiah 39:6-7*

In reviewing Zedekiah's life, we recollect a certain kindness to Jeremiah. When Jeremiah asked him not to return him to the prison house where he would die, Zedekiah agreed. In that manner, Zedekiah saved Jeremiah's life. [75] At that time, he listened to Jeremiah's words:

Jeremiah 34:2-5
"2   Thus saith YeHoVaH, the God of Israel; Go and speak to Zedekiah king of Judah, and tell him, Thus saith YeHoVaH; Behold, I will give this city into the hand of the king of Babylon, and he shall burn it with fire: 3 And thou shalt not escape out of his hand, but shalt surely be taken, and delivered into his hand; and thine eyes shall behold the eyes of the king of Babylon, and he shall speak with thee mouth to mouth, and thou shalt go to Babylon.   4 Yet hear the word of YeHoVaH, O Zedekiah king of Judah; Thus saith YeHoVaH of thee, Thou shalt not die by the sword: 5 [But] thou shalt die in peace: and with the burnings of thy fathers, the former kings which were before thee, so shall they burn [odours] for thee; and they will lament thee, [saying], Ah lord! for I have pronounced the word, saith YeHoVaH. "

Looking at the thirty-month besieging of Jerusalem, and its fall to Nebuchadnezzar, we see every word of Jeremiah regarding Jerusalem's fate transpired exactly

---

[75] *Jeremiah 38:15-26*

as he said. Also, in retrospect, we see the opponents of Jeremiah, along with false prophets and wicked priests, removed from the scene by the hand of YeHoVaH.

It is very possible, many righteous people died in the time of the siege and ransacking of the city. Among the righteous who survive, we have Jeremiah, the prophet, as well as a eunuch in the king's court who was kind to Jeremiah.[76] As Jeremiah looked back on the ashes of this city, and later penned the book of Lamentations, like most true prophets of YeHoVaH, he wept. Such a price paid for rebellion! Such a sad end for those who exchanged the Holy One of Israel for lies, promises and treasures of this world.

Lamentations 4:1-6
> *"1 How is the gold become dim! [how] is the most fine gold changed! the stones of the sanctuary are poured out in the top of every street. 2 The precious sons of Zion, comparable to fine gold, how are they esteemed as earthen pitchers, the work of the hands of the potter! 3 Even the sea monsters draw out the breast, they give suck to their young ones: the daughter of my people [is become] cruel, like the ostriches in the wilderness. 4 The tongue of the sucking child cleaveth to the roof of his mouth for thirst: the young children ask bread, [and] no man breaketh [it] unto them. 5 They that did*

---

[76] *Jeremiah 38:10*

feed delicately are desolate in the streets: they that were brought up in scarlet embrace dunghills. 6 For the punishment of the iniquity of the daughter of my people is greater than the punishment of the sin of Sodom, that was overthrown as in a moment, and no hands stayed on her. "

Let us remember what we have in our God and safeguard it! Let us forsake all that He asks us to forsake and live for Him alone!

"I am crucified with Christ: nevertheless I live; yet not I, but Christ liveth in me: and the life which I now live in the flesh I live by the faith of the Son of God, who loved me, and gave himself for me." [77]

---

[77] *Galatians 2:20*

MATTERS OF
RESTORATION AND RETURN

12

*"For I know the thoughts that I think toward you, saith YeHoVaH, thoughts of peace, and not of evil, to give you an **expected** end."*

Jeremiah 29:11

If there is one thing we can know of a certainty, whether for good or for bad, YeHoVaH keeps His word! Of course, YeHoVaH's greatest desire is that we receive the best from His hand. Thus, He sent His Only begotten Son to the earth to bring us to complete redemption, including the removal of all penalties for sins. [78] This He did out of love for His Creation of mankind, providing for us a way of restoration:

John 3:16
  "16 For God so loved the world, that he gave his only begotten Son, that whosoever believeth in him should not perish, but have everlasting life. "

Likewise, due to His love for Israel, He provided a way of restoration. Information to this restoration shows up primarily in Chapter 33, sandwiched nicely

---

[78] If you are not familiar with this aspect of the faith, turn to the Appendix, to the section entitled "Salvation's Message".

between Judah's judgment and that of the nations around Israel.

Jeremiah 33:3-9

"3 *Call unto me, and I will answer thee, and shew thee great and mighty things, which thou knowest not.* 4 *For thus saith YeHoVaH, the God of Israel, concerning the houses of this city, and concerning the houses of the kings of Judah, which are thrown down by the mounts, and by the sword;* 5 *They come to fight with the Chaldeans, but [it is] to fill them with the dead bodies of men, whom I have slain in mine anger and in my fury, and for all whose wickedness I have hid my face from this city.*

6 *Behold, I will bring it health and cure, and I will cure them, and will reveal unto them the abundance of peace and truth.* 7 *And I will cause the captivity of Judah and the captivity of Israel to return, and will build them, as at the first.* 8 *And I will cleanse them from all their iniquity, whereby they have sinned against me; and I will pardon all their iniquities, whereby they have sinned, and whereby they have transgressed against me.*

9 *And it shall be to me a name of joy, a praise, and an honour before all the nations of the earth, which shall hear all the good that I do unto them: and they shall fear and tremble for all the goodness and for all the prosperity that I procure unto it.* "

158

Here, YeHoVaH promises to answer when they call upon Him. When they do, YeHoVaH promises to show them great and mighty things, of which they know not. Concerning the final days of Jerusalem before its destruction by Babylon, for sure it will happen, however, YeHoVaH promises to bring it health and a cure to the city and its people. He will bring them an abundance of peace and truth.

Here, YeHoVaH promises to bring Judah back from their captivity and on their return, they shall build again, as at the first. In addition, He promises to cleanse them from all their iniquity, whereby they sinned against Him. What an awesome plan to pardon everything whereby they transgressed against Him! Then, to YeHoVaH, Judah becomes a name of joy, which name means praise![79]

Jerusalem, one day, shall be honoured above all nations of the earth. All nations, one day, shall hear the good that YeHoVaH brought to Jerusalem and because of that restoration, they will fear and tremble for all that God lavishes upon Jerusalem.

Jeremiah continues:

---

[79] *Genesis 29:35*

Jeremiah 33:10-13

"10 ¶ Thus saith YeHoVaH; Again there shall be heard in this place, which ye say [shall be] desolate without man and without beast, [even] in the cities of Judah, and in the streets of Jerusalem, that are desolate, without man, and without inhabitant, and without beast, 11 The voice of joy, and the voice of gladness, the voice of the bridegroom, and the voice of the bride, the voice of them that shall say, Praise YeHoVaH of hosts: for YeHoVaH [is] good; for his mercy [endureth] for ever: [and] of them that shall bring the sacrifice of praise into the house of YeHoVaH. For I will cause to return the captivity of the land, as at the first, saith YeHoVaH. 12 Thus saith YeHoVaH of hosts;

Again in this place, which is desolate without man and without beast, and in all the cities thereof, shall be an habitation of shepherds causing [their] flocks to lie down. 13 In the cities of the mountains, in the cities of the vale, and in the cities of the south, and in the land of Benjamin, and in the places about Jerusalem, and in the cities of Judah, shall the flocks pass again under the hands of him that telleth [them], saith YeHoVaH. "

When onlookers see the desolate, deserted, and bleak state of Jerusalem and Judah, where neither man nor beast roam, YeHoVaH promises changes. Indeed, YeHoVaH's ability to restore staggers the mind:

Isaiah 61:1-4

> *"1 The Spirit of the Lord GOD [is] upon me; because YeHoVaH hath anointed me to preach good tidings unto the meek; he hath sent me to bind up the brokenhearted, to proclaim liberty to the captives, and the opening of the prison to [them that are] bound; 2 To proclaim the acceptable year of YeHoVaH, and the day of vengeance of our God; to comfort all that mourn;3 To appoint unto them that mourn in Zion, to give unto them beauty for ashes, the oil of joy for mourning, the garment of praise for the spirit of heaviness; that they might be called trees of righteousness, the planting of YeHoVaH, that he might be glorified. 4 ¶ And they shall build the old wastes, they shall raise up the former desolations, and they shall repair the waste cities, the desolations of many generations. "*

In Jerusalem and the cities of Judah, once again the sound of joy will arise, even great joy at the unifying of two lives together in marriage as family and friends gather to celebrate weddings. Proclamations of praise, once more as in the time of David, arise with phrases like:

"Praise YeHoVaH of hosts: for YeHoVaH [is] good; for his mercy [endureth] for ever".

Indeed, Jerusalem shall enjoy the sacrifice of praise into the house of YeHoVaH, which of course, means it rebuilding.

YeHoVaH promises to return the captivity of the land, meaning He will return to her the freedom He designed for her to enjoy. Once more they will find shepherds with well cared for sheep. These will lie down in their green pastures, content and well fed. What a restoration that promises for all the lands around Jerusalem, including Benjamin, the place where the priests mostly dwelt. Yet, this restoration, so grand and glorious, extends past Judah and Jerusalem. His hand reaches to restore the tribes of the North scattered to the corners of the earth:

Jeremiah 33:14-18
> *"14 Behold, the days come, saith YeHoVaH, that I will perform that good thing which I have promised unto the house of Israel and to the house of Judah. 15 In those days, and at that time, will I cause the Branch of righteousness to grow up unto David; and he shall execute judgment and righteousness in the land. 16 In those days shall Judah be saved, and Jerusalem shall dwell safely: and this [is the name] wherewith she shall be called, YeHoVaH our righteousness. 17 For thus saith YeHoVaH; David shall never want a man to sit upon the throne of the house of Israel; 18 Neither shall the priests the Levites want a man before me to offer*

burnt offerings, and to kindle meat offerings, and to do
sacrifice continually. "

Both houses of Israel and Judah receive restoration.
Looking back on the throne of David, who united both
Judah and Israel, God makes a promise. Even though
many of David's descendants served false gods,
YeHoVaH purifies and returns the kingly line. He
promises to raise up "The Branch of righteousness
unto David"[80]. He executes judgment and
righteousness in the land. When that happens, Judah
shall be saved, and Jerusalem shall dwell safely[81].
Then, Jerusalem shall bear a new name, "YeHoVaH
Tsidkenu" (YeHoVaH our righteousness).

YeHoVaH promises that David shall "never want a
man"[82] to sit upon the throne of the house of Israel.
During the great promised restoration, David's seed
rules over a united Israel, not divided as in the time of
Solomon and onward. Neither shall the priests, the

---

[80] The Messiah

[81] While there is a promised future of this total restoration, in the
meantime, believers who present the gospel to the Jew find a great
reception in these latter days as many Jews are coming to an
awareness that Yeshua was their Messiah. *Isaiah 53*, in its original
Hebrew language makes that so clear! Those who dare to read it
soon discover it! Probably, that's why rabbi's forbade its reading.

[82] Quote from *Jeremiah 33:17-18.*

true Levites, "want a man" before YeHoVaH to offer burnt offerings, and to kindle meat offerings, and to do sacrifice continually.[83]

Just in case there happened to be doubt in the nearby camp of listening ears, YeHoVaH goes one step further:

Jeremiah 33:19-22
"19 And the word of YeHoVaH came unto Jeremiah, saying, 20 Thus saith YeHoVaH; If ye can break my covenant of the day, and my covenant of the night, and that there should not be day and night in their season; 21 [Then] may also my covenant be broken with David my servant, that he should not have a son to reign upon his throne; and with the Levites the priests, my ministers. 22 As the host of heaven cannot be numbered, neither the sand of the sea measured: so will I multiply the seed of David my servant, and the Levites that minister unto me."

Restoration, as God promised, comes! So certain and secure is that promise that YeHoVaH says it fails *only if His People can break His covenant of day and night, so*

---

[83] This restoration's fulfilment comes in the Millennium reign. Both Ezekiel and Jeremiah speak of sacrifices at that time. It could mean a reference to the Temple in their midst, which would be Yeshua, or make reference to something which, at this present time, our minds, due to lack of revelation, just can't quite comprehend.

these no longer exist. If that ever happened, then, no son of David would reign upon the throne. Indeed, the hosts of heaven cannot be numbered, neither the sand of the sea measured, therefore, YeHoVaH's promises to multiply the seed of David, and those that minister unto Him in righteousness, will see their fulfilment.

As fantastic as these promises seem, God has more awaiting. He says consider this:

Jeremiah 33:23-26
> *"23 Moreover the word of YeHoVaH came to Jeremiah, saying, 24 Considerest thou not what this people have spoken, saying, The two families which YeHoVaH hath chosen, he hath even cast them off? thus they have despised my people, that they should be no more a nation before them. 25 Thus saith YeHoVaH; If my covenant [be] not with day and night, [and if] I have not appointed the ordinances of heaven and earth; 26 Then will I cast away the seed of Jacob, and David my servant, [so] that I will not take [any] of his seed [to be] rulers over the seed of Abraham, Isaac, and Jacob: for I will cause their captivity to return, and have mercy on them. "*

Never, ever, will YeHoVaH cast away the seed of Jacob, (Israel) and David His servant. Indeed, YeHoVaH causes their captivity to return, and has mercy on them.

FURTHER RESTORATION:

In reading Jeremiah, Chapter 31 promises the restoration of a new (renewed) covenant. That promise reads:

Jeremiah 31:31-34

"31 *Behold, the days come, saith YeHoVaH, that I will make a new[84] covenant with the house of Israel, and with the house of Judah: 32 Not according to the covenant that I made with their fathers in the day [that] I took them by the hand to bring them out of the land of Egypt; which my covenant they brake, although I was an husband unto them, saith YeHoVaH: 33 But this [shall be] the covenant that I will make with the house of Israel; After those days, saith YeHoVaH, I will put my law in their inward parts, and write it in their hearts; and will be their God, and they shall be my people. 34 And they shall teach no more every man his neighbour, and every man his brother, saying, Know YeHoVaH: for they shall all know me, from the least of them unto the greatest of them, saith YeHoVaH: for I will forgive their iniquity, and I will remember their sin no more. "*

---

[84] This word means "renewed". It is the same word used to speak of a new moon appearing in the sky monthly. That moon is not newly created! It is renewed. Please keep this in mind, as YeHoVaH never casts away His People! He renews His covenant with them!

166

This restoration touches deep! It reaches the inner part
of man where the source of disobedience lives. Into
this place of the heart, the source of all choices,
YeHoVaH carves His Laws and precepts! Therefore,
the keeping of His commandments comes forth to the
delight of His heart. That is awesome restoration! That
is the beauty and amazement of the "renewed
covenant" promised by Jeremiah, and as Christians
believe, fulfilled in Yeshua.

RETURN:

In 1948 Israel returned to her homeland, and since that
time Jews from all around the world returned to live in
the land of their forefathers. They buy and sell land,
just as Jeremiah predicted[85]! Jerusalem, today, is once
again a beautiful city with paved streets, markets,
businesses, and technological enterprises, which
regularly astound the world around them.[86]

Israel's government functions as a democracy, blessing
the people with the rights and freedoms as scripture
defines. Israel's army stands equipped and ready to
protect their land from invaders, and while Israel,
presently, lives in peace, she is surrounded by

---

[85] *Jeremiah 32:7-8; Jeremiah 32:42-44*
[86] If you wish to do a little research, study, and see how many
modern inventions originate from the Jewish mind.

countries which hate her, and regularly promise to destroy her.

Yet, those promises, unfulfilled, fall to the ground for Israel shall stand as God decrees!

As far as a total peace extending to every nook and cranny of Israel, time awaits its fulfilment as does the return of the Messiah. We must remember that just as God's promises for Israel's return to her own land took centuries, it nevertheless came to pass. Likewise, the remaining passages of scripture pertinent to Israel's full restoration,[87] also, shall come to pass. YeHoVaH's mighty hand brings it to pass, in His time and season.

---

[87] All promises in the Word of God come to pass, whether it is regarding Israel or any other nation. God's Word never fails!

CONCLUSION

"10 I have seen the travail, which God hath given to the sons of men to be exercised in it."

"11 ¶ He hath made every thing beautiful in his time: also he hath set the world in their heart, so that no man can find out the work that God maketh from the beginning to the end. 12 I know that there is no good in them, but for a man to rejoice, and to do good in his life. 13 And also that every man should eat and drink, and enjoy the good of all his labour, it is the gift of God. 14 I know that, whatsoever God doeth, it shall be for ever: nothing can be put to it, nor any thing taken from it: and God doeth it, that men should fear before him. 15 That which hath been is now; and that which is to be hath already been; and God requireth that which is past."

"16 ¶ And moreover I saw under the sun the place of judgment, that wickedness was there; and the place of righteousness, that iniquity was there. 17 I said in mine heart, God shall judge the righteous and the wicked: for there is a time there for every purpose and for every work."

Ecclesiastes 3:10-17

169

Solomon, in reflecting the seasons of life, included the place of judgment. He saw wickedness in the place where judgment occurred. He saw iniquity where righteousness should operate.[88] As he pondered these things, perhaps wondering at their existence, he said in his heart, "God shall judge the righteous and the wicked", and concluded again, there is a time for every purpose and for every work".

There are seasons in everyone's lifetime when they ask, "why do certain things happen?". Some generations fought world wars while others enjoyed peacetime. Some generations saw God's Laws obeyed in their land; others saw rebellion. Some generations saw democratic societies, others saw dictatorships. The list goes on for things that generations experienced in the various nations of the world.

Whatever the season the generation experienced, it was theirs to discern and theirs to challenge or support. Regarding the gospel, and the truth of the scriptures,

---

[88] Biblically speaking, *"wickedness in the place of judgment"* refers to rulership in the courts of the land. *"Iniquity in the place of righteousness"* refers to the House of God, where spiritual rulership took place. In modern terms, our governments, when functioning as God designed, bring true justice. Churches, when functioning as God designed, operate in a spiritual authority where righteousness abounds. At least, that is God's plan, so the question remains: how do we measure up?

it, also, was theirs to believe and propagate believers, or theirs to let fall to the ground. Each generation, each season under heaven, gives an account to the Living God for their behaviour.

Jeremiah, in his time upon the earth, God did not permit him to marry. Thus, he had had no legacy, no children to carry on his name. This action demonstrated by this sign prophet speaks loudly. His generation was the last one before judgment! In other words, no other generation followed that of Jeremiah in Jerusalem at that time. Jerusalem, for a season, lay barren, desolate, and uninhabited, a recipient of God's judgment.

So dear one, as you look at the times and seasons in which you live, you discern the place and season of your nation before God. You spend time with the Almighty and you analyze both your nation in its place before God, and your part in your society, in the season in which God planted you! Think about God's call for righteousness to all generations and see how your generation measures up on God's scale of justice.

As you do, contemplate the need to speak out like Jeremiah, the necessity for God's voice of life and love to a lost generation. Could God be calling you to be such a voice? If so, remember, He is calling you, also, to cry out to Him for mercy for them, to seek His Face

171

for His Spirit's conviction to move across your nation, giving people opportunity to repent.

Also, remember, God verifies His Word in His prophet's mouth, either by witnesses of earth or by times and seasons fulfilled. *Remember, a true prophet's call is to see people return to God!*

In Jeremiah 18 we see a troubled nation in need of repentance, a nation gone their own direction away from God. As the potter's wheel spun and as his hands shaped the vessel, the vessel became marred. Displeased with the vessel, the potter made the vessel over again. Then, after Jeremiah's first-hand experience with the potter and his wheel, the Word of YeHoVaH came to Jeremiah:

Jeremiah 18:6
"6 O house of Israel, cannot I do with you as this potter? saith YeHoVaH. Behold, as the clay [is] in the potter's hand, so [are] ye in mine hand, O house of Israel."

Just like the pot formed on the wheel of the potter, YeHoVaH formed Israel. He shaped her to be a holy vessel unto Him, giving her laws, commandments, and precepts to follow, so she would stand for righteousness, and thus, be a beacon light for all nations to see.

However, Israel did her own thing. That self-willed behaviour, YeHoVaH compared to a marred vessel, a piece of clay that refused to be shaped as the maker intended. No one questioned the potter's right to reshape the marred vessel! Why can YeHoVaH, therefore, the creator and redeemer of Israel, not do as He must do to shape the vessel His way?

YeHoVaH then goes on to speak about nations:

Jeremiah 18:7-10
"7 [At what] instant I shall speak concerning a nation, and concerning a kingdom, to pluck up, and to pull down, and to destroy [it]; 8 If that nation, against whom I have pronounced, turn from their evil, I will repent of the evil that I thought to do unto them. 9 And [at what] instant I shall speak concerning a nation, and concerning a kingdom, to build and to plant [it]; 10 If it do evil in my sight, that it obey not my voice, then I will repent of the good, wherewith I said I would benefit them."

YeHoVaH, owns the sovereign right to pluck up, pull down, destroy, and totally remove any nation on the face of the earth. However, if that nation, slotted for removal, repents, and turns away from their evil, God's heart towards them shifts away from needed judgment and moves towards blessing.

Likewise, if a nation determined by God to be built and planted, turns against God's ways, God's heart towards that nation can shift away from blessing to judgment.

Armed with this lesson from the potter's house, YeHoVaH sent Jeremiah to speak again to His people:

> Jeremiah 18:11
> "11¶ Now therefore go to, speak to the men of Judah, and to the inhabitants of Jerusalem, saying, Thus saith YeHoVaH; Behold, I frame evil against you, and devise a device against you: return ye now every one from his evil way, and make your ways and your doings good."

Any nation, no matter its original foundation, development, or function, stands before YeHoVaH. He is the Judge of all the earth! Let a nation of evil roots repent and turn for good, God will bless them. Let a good nation turn away from God and refuse to repent and return, God's judgment comes. This is the lesson learned at the potter's house by Jeremiah.

Believers must learn to embrace that lesson. We must realize that YeHoVaH has a message for every nation under heaven. He still rewards good and distains evil. Time does not change YeHoVaH![89] However, out of mercy, YeHoVaH prefers to release blessings, rather

---

[89] *Malachi 3:6*

than judgment and therefore, He trains prophets and sends them to all nations of the world with the same basic message: REPENT. [90]

Whatever your call, whatever your situation, do remember Jeremiah! Remember what price that prophet paid to see the Word of God go forth in his generation, and in his land. Remember his deep love for God, and the people, even the ones who opposed him. Depend upon the Almighty to set your heart like a flint towards righteousness and truth, expressing His heart of love to all, even those who await His hand of judgment!

Remember, God's promise to make Jeremiah a brazen wall, a fortified city to withstand the resistance against them. Remember the depth of the word promised no escape from struggles, physical or otherwise! God promised to keep Jeremiah through it all, helping him not to succumb to that which aimed at taking his soul! YeHoVaH helped Jeremiah to stay faithful to his God, not moved by his circumstances.

Jeremiah's life, preserved by YeHoVaH, saw his destiny fulfilled and his end, although tragic, brought him into the realms of glory with the One to Whom he served and loved with every breath of his being.

---

[90] Missionaries go out to speak the message of truth. In that way they speak for God and qualify as a prophet sent to a nation.

Dear one, no matter your generation, *even if it is the Jeremiah generation,* (the one in which God's judgment falls), carefully weigh out the costs before God, *before you speak for Him.*[91] He knows the ones He formed in their mother's womb to be a voice to each generation. Remember also, only God knows how your generation receives His Word! He alone knows, ahead of time, who will repent and return to Him! It might be that your generation becomes a repenting generation that returns to God!

So, if God calls you to speak for Him, ensure, first, that you are securely plugged into heaven and to its power source. Then, move throughout your generation with all the power of God behind you. Experience what God can do through an obedient, willing vessel called to speak for Him!

Remember, with God, all things are possible.

Mark 9:23
*"Jesus said unto him, If thou canst believe, all things are **possible** to him that believeth. "*

---

[91] *Luke 14:25-33*

APPENDIX

A Name to Honour

יְהֹוָה

YeHoVaH[92]

If, today, someone asked you to tell them the name of your earthly father, without hesitation you would declare it. If, for some reason, you did not know the identity of your earthly father, you would say so. You might even give an explanation as to why that might be so. Thus said, if asked to relate the name of your heavenly Father, today, would you do so with ease, or would you draw a blank?

Most of Christendom, today, seem unknowing as to the name of the Father. As the author of this book, I would like to join the ranks of those who wish to relate that name to the world as an honour to our God. When we stand before Him on the day we give an account for

---

[92] Based on information given by Michael Rood. Some from his work entitled, The Chronological Bible, and some from his YouTube videos. For more information see page 28 of the Chronological Bible.

our deeds in this body, it would be a good thing to have known Him, and used His Name, often.

Did you know that the name of the Father appears at least 6,828 times in the Hebrew scriptures? Scribes recorded it with four specific Hebrew letters. They are as follows:

י	Pronounced yode, or yod
ה	Pronounced as hey
ו	Pronounced as vav
ה	Pronounced as hey

For centuries, whenever the Jews came across these four Hebrew letters they simply said, Adonai, or Ha Shem (meaning the name). They refused then, and most today, to pronounce the name for several reasons, some of which we will look at momentarily. For now, let us look at whether their tradition affected Christianity. That we can easily do by looking at our Bibles to see the four-letter name of the Father either written or substituted.

A quick look reveals that our KVJ Bibles, as well as many other versions, the four-letter name presented to readers is a four-letter English word, "LORD" [93].

---

[93] In some translations it is GOD.

Whether intentional or not, Christendom has followed the ancient tradition of the Jews.

An Ancient Tradition

In early second century times[94] Rabbis hid the pronunciation of the holy name of God. They did this by omitting the vowel pointings, which are necessary to make the name pronounceable. Hence, as they carefully wrote the scriptures, their omittance of the vowel pointings made the name unpronounceable. Historians believe there were two reasons why they did this:

i.   According to Josephus, Rome, under the rule of Domitian, 81 to 96 CE, put to death anyone using the name of the Jewish or Christian God.

ii. Many believe that the Rabbis borrowed a tradition from pagans, whereby the name of their god was considered too holy to mention, so they called him "Ba-al" meaning Lord. The Jews adopted this practice and most still practice it today, even some Messianic Jews!

Tradition Continues

Bible translators followed their tradition for many reasons, which are not presently known. It is possible

---

[94] Some scholars believe it to date even further back.

but doubtful that they forgot the pronunciation of the name, but it seems more than likely that due to present day thinking, those who knew it, hid it.[95]. Whatever the reason, following this tradition of the Jews, additionally, caused Christians to continue it.

Does that tradition offend

the Heavenly Father?

If indeed its origin was Baal worship, then we can give a resounding Amen to the fact it offends God. In addition, as we look at scripture, we see the Almighty was not pleased with this, for His Heart desires all to enjoy salvation, including the Gentiles. How can that happen if they do not know upon what name they should call? Scripture [96] clearly says in the end times, Gentiles will know His name and call upon it to receive salvation. Obviously, for that to happen, they must know the name of YeHoVaH (יְהוָֹה).

An Historic Discovery

Today, some Hebrew scholars[97] have searched the world over for Hebrew manuscripts. In doing so, they

---

[95] According to some, the Jews secretly knew the name.

[96] *Jeremiah 16:1-2*

[97] Nehemiah Gordon, a Hebrew scholar, according to his testimony, found the name of the Father with all vowel pointings in the Aleppo Codex, and through his efforts, and those of others

found many Hebrew documents have the full name with vowels and therefore the pronunciation of the name. These scholars may different slightly in pronunciation, but nevertheless, they are making the name of YeHoVaH known today.

OUR SAVIOUR'S NAME HIDDEN IN THIS NAME

In looking at the Hebrew root of the name of the Father, pronounced *Yah-Ho **Vah'***, and looking at another scripture, we see something amazing about our Saviour. In speaking of the Prophet, the one the Father would send and to whom all must listen and obey, YeHoVaH said that His name would be in the name of the Prophet.

Exodus 23:21 "Beware of him, and obey his voice, provoke him not; for he will not pardon your transgressions[98]: for my name [is] in him."

Our Saviour's name, as given by the angel was "Yehoshua", which means Salvation.

That name, with its Hebrew letters reads as:

י	**Pronounced yode or yod**
ה	**Pronounced hey**

---

discovered that name with vowel pointings in over 2000 manuscripts.

[98] Please keep in mind that Yeshua bore the punishment for your sins. Your sins were not pardoned, they were atoned!

ו	Pronounced vav
שׁ	Pronounced shin
ע	Pronounced ayin

The name of the Father (יְהֹוָה) is in the name of the Son! The first three letters of YeHoVaH show it! (Yod, Heh, Vav). Is it so amazing that the name of our Father is in the true name of the One YeHoVaH sent to redeem us!

Honour the Father's Name

Throughout this book, and all later books, as well as all accompanying audios and PowerPoints, it is the author's intention to widely use, proclaim and continually pronounce the name of the Father, as well as the name of Yeshua. Indeed, this breaks with tradition of many, however, thus far as we have shared the news of the Father's name and use Yeshua's birth name, reception has been excellent.

YeHoVaH's Name Challenge

Since, as of this reading, you are no longer ignorant of your heavenly Father's name, we invite you to join the unofficial network of proclaimers of the Father's name and shout it from the house tops. In doing so, you honour the Heavenly Father, our Saviour Yeshua, and the Holy Spirit.

Romans 10:12-15

"12   For there is no difference between the Jew and the Greek: for the same Lord over all is rich unto all that call upon him. 13 For whosoever shall call upon the name of the Lord shall be saved. 14 How then shall they call on him in whom they have not believed? and how shall they believe in him of whom they have not heard? and how shall they hear without a preacher? 15 And how shall they preach, except they be sent? as it is written, How beautiful are the feet of them that preach the gospel of peace, and bring glad tidings of good things!"

ABOUT THE KING JAMES VERSION

Scriptures quoted in this book *originate* from the KJV **public domain version** of the Bible, which means, no copyright exists on this version of the scripture. While some find this translation outdated, Jeanne, trained in the KJV still finds this version helpful, and uses it in all her books[99].

In using KJV, however, it is good to remember the following:

- *Some words in the KJV have changed meaning over the centuries. To understand such words, look up the root word in its original language. In doing so, the meaning stands out. For example. KJV uses the word "conversation" however, in its original language it means moral character, or behaviour.*
- *When KJV spoke of humanity, they said, "man". When you read that word, or hear others speak about the scriptures using the term, "man", know it refers to all humankind, not a specific gender.*

Due to tradition, the name of the Father, YeHoVaH appears as LORD, or at times as Jehovah. However, in all CP &AA's manuscripts, YeHoVaH's (or YHVH) replaces the term LORD.

---

[99] In later manuscripts, the author updated the more archaic words in the KJV such as wouldest or couldest.

SALVATION'S MESSAGE

Yeshua, when walking on earth, said this:

> *John 3:14-18*
> *"14 And as Moses lifted up the serpent in the wilderness, even so must the Son of man be lifted up: 15 That whosoever believes in him should not perish but have eternal life. 16 For God so loved the world, that he gave his only begotten Son, that whosoever believes in him should not perish, but have everlasting life. 17 For God sent not his Son into the world to condemn the world; but that the world through him might be saved. 18 He that believes on him is not condemned: but he that believes not is condemned already, because he hath not believed in the name of the only begotten Son of God. "*

During the time of Moses, the children of Israel, in the wilderness, rebelled against God, at which time poisonous serpents infiltrated the camp, killing many of the people. After seeking YeHoVaH for a solution to the problem, Moses followed God's instructions and made a bronze serpent fashioned and erected it on a pole in sight of the people. Whosoever wanted to live, must acknowledge their rebellion against YeHoVaH, and in doing so, look upon the erected pole and bronze serpent, to YeHoVaH, who gave them life in place of death, then they would live.

Yeshua said, just as Moses erected that bronze serpent in the wilderness, He would be lifted up. This referred to the event, in the future, of Yeshua's crucifixion. During the time when the serpent hung on that pole, whosoever wanted to live and not die from the serpent's bite must acknowledge their rebellion, their sin against YeHoVaH.

Likewise, for those who wish to live eternally, they must look upon the cross of the crucified One, to YeHoVaH, who provided life for them. This was an act of love for all humankind, necessary because man is born from Adam, and thus is born with an inherent sin.

Secondly, man sins. The consequence of sin is death, and eternal death, wherein man will spend an eternity in darkness, away from YeHoVaH. Unfortunately, there is nothing humanly possible to reverse those consequences. Even if a person had made a genuine decision never to sin again, and for some reason they succeeded, all their good deeds and good living would not erase the penalty of eternal death.

There is only *one way* for Eternal Life to touch a person's life. That way Yeshua explained to His listeners as *through the cross.*

Salvation comes by understanding these facts:

1. Yeshua, being the Son of God and the fulfilment of the scriptures, never sinned.
2. YeHoVaH, on behalf of every human being on the earth, chose to make Yeshua become as sin, in His Eyes, so that Yeshua might pay the penalty for sin, for all of humanity.
3. Yeshua paid that penalty. He died on the cross and was buried in a tomb.
4. Three days later, He rose again, appearing to His disciples, to show them the reality of His resurrection, to show them God vindicated Him and made Him both Lord and Messiah.
5. Yeshua could not stay in the tomb, because "death" comes to all who sin, but since Yeshua never sinned, therefore, death could not hold Him in the grave.
6. All those who come to Yeshua, to receive Him as their Saviour, receive liberty from sin and from its horrible consequence, eternal death.
7. They enter YeHoVaH's Kingdom and receive eternal life, as well as another gift: **The Righteousness of Messiah.** After salvation, when YeHoVaH looks upon a believer in Messiah, He sees Yeshua's perfect life and sees a redeemed believer, set aside for YeHoVaH. Since salvation has taken place in the believer, the Holy Spirit dwells within them.
8. All it takes to receive salvation from YeHoVaH is receiving His Messiah, fully repenting from

sinning against God[100]. YeHoVaH even gives the believer the faith to receive His gift of Salvation!

The Apostle Paul put it this way:

Ephesians 2:8
"For by grace are ye saved through faith; and that not of yourselves: it is the gift of God"

When you pray the following prayer, realize we present it here to get you started in your walk with YeHoVaH. Living out your salvation depends upon your commitment to follow through from this point, onward. *From the moment of your commitment and onward, dear one, please seek YeHoVaH for His help in all things, including help to make your life align with truth, and in the end be a praise unto His name, forever!*

---

[100] And against man. When a person steals, etc. they sin against both God and man. PLEASE NOTE: all references to "man", either by scripture or the author, refers to all humankind, not a specific gender.

SINNER'S PRAYER

& LIFETIME COMMITMENT

Heavenly, Father:

I acknowledge before You, Lord, that I am a sinner. I understand sin's punishment is a life without You, for all eternity. Thank You for sending Yeshua to the earth, as the Messiah. I understand now that He died in my place, to take my punishment for my sins. I believe You raised Yeshua from the dead, and now that I accepted Him as my personal Saviour, my old life dies, and my new life begins.

I humbly ask You, Lord, to forgive me of my sins, and as of this moment, I receive Yeshua as my Mashiach. I open my heart to receive the works of the cross that You provided for me through Yeshua, and with Your help, I will walk away from my sin, turning my back upon my own will and ways. I will now live my life seeking to obey Your Word and Your will. Help me to live, from this point onward, in a manner pleasing to You.

One more thing:

Remember, this gospel message comes with power. When you hear it, the Kingdom of God draws near to you. When you repent of your sins and receive salvation, the Kingdom of God moves within. You cannot see it, feel it, or tell it from an outward observance. It is accepted, received, and lived out by faith! Seek out other believers in Messiah and may God bless you richly as you live your life, now, completely for Him!

So now, be sure and tell someone!

Remember that a person believes with the heart unto righteousness and confesses with their mouth unto salvation, as spoken about in *Romans 10:10, which says, "For with the heart man believes unto righteousness; and with the mouth confession is made unto salvation"*.

SCRIPTURE INDEX

OTHER BOOKS BY THIS AUTHOR

An Arsenal of Powerful Prayers [101]
  Scriptural Prayers to Move Mountains
Arising Incense
  A Believer's Priesthood
Above Artificial Intelligence
  Finding God in a World of A.I.
Bible Study Basics
  A Closer Look at God's Word
Candidate for A Miracle
  Wisdom from the Miracles of Yeshua
Foundations of Revival
  Biblical Evidence for Revival
His Reflection
  What God longs to see in His People
Heaven's Greater Government
  Behind the Scenes of Earth's Events
In The Name of Yehovah
  Biblical use of Banners
It's All About Heaven
  As Pictured in Scripture
Kingdom Keys for Kingdom Kids
  Walking in Kingdom Power
Molded for the Miraculous
  Why God made You

---

[101] This is a book of written prayers of assorted topics to help believers live a stronger, active faith. No workbook.

Our Secure Faith Heritage

Foundational Truths to an Unshakeable Walk with God

Releasing the Impossible

The Limitless Power of Intercession

Volume 1: Intercessions from the Author's Life

Volume 2: Intercessions from Biblical Characters

Workbook: Both Volumes compiled in Workbook.

Salvation Depicted in a Meal [102]

An Hebraic Christian Guide to Passover

The Jeremiah Generation

God's Response to Injustice

The Warrior Bride-

God's Kingdom Advancing through Spiritual Warfare

Thy Kingdom Come

Entering God's Rest in Prayer

Watching, Waiting, Warning

Obeying Yeshua's Command to Watch & Pray

When Nations Rumble

A Study of the Book of Amos

Worship in Spirit and In Truth [103]

The Tabernacle of David - Past, Present & Future

---

[102] Haggadah (Guide) for a Christian Passover. No Workbook.

[103] Good sister book to "In the Name of YeHoVaH We Set Up Our Banners".

ABOUT JEANNE METCALF

Jeanne believes the Word of God opens a door to help every believer to know their God. That knowledge, once gleaned and retained, makes strong believers to help them stand in the real world in which we live, no matter their vocation.

With these convictions in mind, Jeanne, inspired and led by the Holy Spirit, began to write in the 1990's. Soon she developed inductive[104] style Bible Studies and self-published them for her students to use. With her major goal to equip the saints, she found that her sound teachings, presented with clarity and simplicity, made an impact. As long as her listeners put in their valuable time to study scripture and took Jeanne's advice to call upon the Holy Spirit to help them, they became powerful believers, transformed, prepared and ready to stand in their generation.

Today, past students who studied the Bible with Jeanne, as well current new students, testify as to the validity of Jeanne's writing and teaching gift. They

---

[104] In the inductive Bible Study method, believers learn first by reading and studying the Word on their own, then they glean from the textbook. This study method often gives a better foundation to a believer's faith than sitting through lectures or speaker related teachings.

199

love the clarity and simplicity of the Word as she presents it in a refreshing straightforward format. Thus, they encouraged Jeanne to make her books more widely available.

Therefore, Jeanne began Cegullah Publishing, and then a year later, opened Cegullah Apologetic Academy. The academy, in addition to presenting accredited, Bible Study material, invites all believers to read or study the Word of God, and thereby, be strong in YeHoVaH and the strength of His might.

A greater availability of Jeanne's works (as well as other authors which Cegullah Publishing looks forward to publishing in the future), opens doors for more people to know their God and do exploits!

"But the people that know their God shall be strong and do exploits". Daniel 11:32 b

***

About CP & AA
CEGULLAH PUBLISHING & APOLOGETICS ACADEMY.

We are an accredited academy, who publishes books. Since the content we publish is based upon the Bible, the Word of God, we consider our books treasures. Through these available treasures, we give opportunities for our reading audience to explore pertinent topics which steady, reaffirm, and help them to walk out their life in victory.

Our Vision
- To supply Christian, Bible-based materials to help readers study God's Word

Our Focus
- To help our readers to know **what they believe and why.**

Our Mission
- To provide bible studies, devotionals, teachings, and other educational tools to help readers to know their God and connect with Him.

Our Publishing Motto:
- *Publishing the treasures of modern-day scribes.*

Our Academy Motto:
- *Earnestly contend for the faith once given to the saints.*

CONTACT INFORMATION

www.cegullahpublishing.ca